Travel guide to
NORWAY

TABLE OF CONTENTS

Publisher: © **Pictura Normann AS**
Postbox 223, N-2001 Lillestrøm
Tel: +47 64802700 - Fax: +47 64802701
www.normanns.no - Email: normanns@normanns.no

Nærøyfjorden, typical scenery in Western Norway.

WELCOME TO NORWAY!

A legend from the time of the Vikings tells of the wild and beautiful princess Skade who was living happily on the island of Zealand. One day an ancient god demanded her hand in marriage and her parents dared not but go along with his demand. Skade did not want to marry him, and decided to flee. She crossed the Baltic sea and hid in a secluded meadow in Skandia, where, according to the legend, she still lives out in nature, still as beautiful, free and happy. If we put the word Skade together with Auia, which means "meadow" in the Viking language, we get the word Skadeauia or "Skade meadow," Europe's last natural paradise.

Scandinavia extends over a large area on the earth's northern hemisphere and covers approximately 4% of the earth's surface. The area has approx. 25 million inhabitants and consists of Norway, Sweden and Denmark. Because of its location, people often tend to include Iceland and Finland, however the proper designation for that is the Nordic countries. We have the Gulf Stream to thank for Scandinavia's climate. The warm climate along the Nordic coast is an important prerequisite for plants, animals and humans. Without this life-giving force would, Scandinavia today would be an arctic wasteland of tundra and ice.

Norway, the way towards the North

The name Norway already existed very long ago as "Norvegr" or the North way. The name was later used for 500 years by pilgrims who came from all over Northern Europe who set

NORGE

NORDAUSTLANDET

BARENTSØYA

SPITZBERGEN

EDGEØYA

SVALBARD

NORDKAPP   HONNINGSVÅG

HAMMERFEST   VARDØ

TROMSØ   ALTA   KIRKENES

KARASJOK

I. VESTERALEN   ANDENES   KAUTOKEINO   **ROSSIJA**

NORSKEHAVET

I. LOFOTEN   NARVIK

SVOLVÆR

BODØ   FAUSKE

POLARSIRKEL

MO I RANA

TRONDHEIM   **SVERIGE**   **SUOMI**

ÅLESUND   ÅNDALSNES

GEIRANGER   DOMBÅS

BALESTRAND

SOGNETJOLD   VOSS

BERGEN

KONGSBERG   LILLEHAMMER

STAVANGER   SKIEN   **OSLO**

MOSS

FREDRIKSTAD   **ESTLAND**

LARVIK   *B A L T I S K E*

ARENDAL   *S J Ø*

MANDAL   KRISTIANSAND

DANMARK

TYSKLAND   **POLEN**

out on the "way towards the North" for a visit to the grave of St. Olav in Nidaros Cathedral in Nidaros, now Trondheim.

Norway consists of long, relatively high ridges and deep valleys stretching north. It is one of the world's northernmost countries, from the 58° north at Lindesnes to 71° north at the North Cape, and 81° north at Svalbard. With its 385.455 km², it is the fifth largest country in Europe (Russia and Turkey not included). From Lindesnes to Kinnarodden (south-north) there is a distance of 1752 km. From the Swedish border in the east to the North Sea in the west, the longest distance is 430 km,

Geirangerfjorden is one of Norway's biggest tourist attractions.

The midnight sun at the North Cape.

whereas at Hellemobotn in Tysfjord it is only six miles from the coast to the Swedish border.

Norway is bordered by Sweden, Finland and Russia.

Norway has some of the most stunning scenery to offer. Year after year, thousands of tourists come to admire its unique nature. It is so magnificent, beautiful and fascinating that residents say that this is nature's gift. Norway is the land of fjords, valleys and mountains, with Europe's largest mainland glaciers and vast forests. In northern Norway, northern lights dance in winter and in summer, the midnight sun shines. The country has about. 5 million inhabitants, with a population density of less than 14 inh/km². The country also has a Sami minority of approx. 40,000 who live in the north. The main cities are the capital Oslo, Bergen, Trondheim, Stavanger and Tromsø. The country is divided into 19 counties, and these again into 429 municipalities.

There is freedom of religion in Norway, but 79% of the population belongs to the Evangelical-Lutheran state church, although only about 3% are regular churchgoers.

The country has two official forms of Norwegian: Bokmål and Nynorsk. In addition, Sami is the official language in many municipalities in the north. Norway is a constitutional monarchy, King Harald V and Queen Sonja are the country's royal couple.

Parliament has 169 members from all over the country.

History

Norway's history as a nation begins with the Vikings. That period lasted about 250 years, from 793 to 1066. The Norwegian Vikings were without a doubt the most adventurous of the Scandinavians. They opened trade routes, embarked on raids across the North Sea, and travelled to Ireland, Scotland, France, Galicia in northern Spain and the Mediterranean. They

Lofoten in Northern Norway.

also crossed the Atlantic, populated Island and travelled to Greenland and Canada 500 years before Columbus discovered America.

The Norwegian kings, such as Harald Fairhair and Olav Tryggvason, always dreamed of uniting the country under one rule. But it was Olav Haraldsson who finally managed to do so. He introduced an administrative system, and converted the Vikings to Christianity. When Olaf Haraldsson died in the Battle of Stiklestad in 1030 and was buried as St. Olav in Nidaros church in Trondheim, the fabled Viking era came to an end. Nidaros church became the symbol of the country's Christian assembly. Norway was an independent kingdom when it was unified under Harald Fairhair in 872 In 1319, the last king of the Fairhair lineage died without leaving a male heir. Norway and Sweden formed their first union, which was later joined by Denmark. At this time,

people made pilgrimages to St. Olav's tomb. As a result of the Reformation, Protestantism was introduced in 1536.

Norway was under Danish rule until 1814. After a brief period as an independent kingdom with its own constitution (one of the oldest), the country entered into a union with Sweden. Politicians, artists such as Grieg and Ibsen and society made an effort to strengthen the Norwegian national sentiment. In 1905, the union was dissolved, and Norway was once again an independent nation. Prince Carl of Denmark was crowned as the Norwegian king at Nidaros cathedral under the name of Håkon VII.

During World War II, Norway was occupied by the Germans. The king formed a government in exile in London. Resistance was active in the fight against the Germans. The German occupation lasted until

1945, and had very tragic results for the country, such as repression and the destruction of large parts of northern Norway, and the losses of the merchant marine. Two episodes should be mentioned in connection to this: the Battle of Narvik, the Allied forces' first victory over the Axis forces and the fight for heavy water. The fight for heavy water occurred in Telemark, and prevented - so it was thought at the time - the Germans from being able to develop the atomic bomb.

Today, Norway is a modern country, which, thanks to oil, has the third highest per capita income in the world after Switzerland and Luxembourg. According to the UN, Norway is the best country in which to live.

The Economy

When Norway became an independent nation in 1905, it was one of the world's poorest countries, mainly inhabited by farmers and fishermen. Today, one century later, it is one of the wealthiest, thanks to the oil and gas discoveries on the Norwegian continental shelf. Norway is the world's second largest oil exporter after OPEC.

The major oil fields, located between the coast of Scotland and the south-eastern part of Norway, produces approx. 2 million barrels a day. Of these, 10% goes to national consumption. The rest is exported, mostly to European countries. Rogaland, along with the city Stavanger, is the centre for this great activity, and the state company Statoil controls all operations associated with the "black gold".

Norway has a coastline of over 21,000 km and the world's fifth largest fishing fleet, along with a very well developed fishing industry of open sea fishing, and the production of canned and frozen fish products. There is also a strong increase in fish farming.

The eternal snow and the more

Oil platform at Stavanger.

Besseggen in South Norway.

than 1,600 glaciers that exist in the country, produce a large amount of hydropower that Norway partly exports to its neighbouring countries. Norway is also a major producer of aluminium thanks to the availability of cheap electric power. The country has mines and large factories which played an important part in its industrialization process in the last century.

Only 2.8% of the country's surface area is arable land. The majority of agricultural products that are consumed must therefore be imported. Apples and strawberries that are grown in Norway are very tasty thanks to the microclimates in many places in the Norwegian fjords. In recent years, tourism has become one of the major industries in Norway.

Art

With its Viking past and its beautiful nature, Norway has provided major contributions to the history of art. The works of the great Norwegian artists, such as Vigeland, Munch, Ibsen and Grieg, have helped to define the Norwegian soul and to establish the pillars of the nation.

One of Norway's most important contributions in architecture are the stave churches. They are built of wood and mark the transition from paganism to Christianity, and therefore also have decorative items from Viking beliefs: dragon heads, shell-like roofs, intertwining snakes and masks. The name stave is the construction method based on vertically standing wooden staves in contrast to log buildings where the walls are formed by horizontally lying timber. In the Middle Ages, there were more than a thousand stave churches in Norway, but since that time many of them have been destroyed by fire and the ravages of time. Most were simply torn down in the second half of the 1800s, because they were too small, draughty and uncomfortable.

Today only about 30 stave churches remain. These are protected by law as art treasures. Some of the most notable are Borgund in Laerdal, which is the best preserved, Gol Stave Church which stands at the Folk Museum in Oslo, and Urnes Stave Church in the Sognefjord, which is the oldest. as well as the stave church in Heddal Telemark (the world's largest stave church), nicknamed "the stave Cathedral". The stave churches, represented by Urnes, were added to UNESCO's "cultural heritage of the world" list, on which Norway is also represented by Bryggen in Bergen, the wooden house town of Røros, the petroglyph fields in Alta, Vega Island, the Western Norwegian fjords with the Geiranger fjord and Nærøy fjord and the Struve Geodetic Arc - the four Norwegian points.

In sculpture, Gustav Vigeland is Norway's best-known exponent. Most of his works are in Frogner Park in Oslo, also referred to as Vigeland Park. A compilation of 671 characters create an impressive reflection on human life and death. The force, gravity and humanity in the Vigeland sculptures make a very deep impression.

There is no doubt that a country with such beautiful nature would also produce huge artists. Johan Christian Clausen Dahl is one of the best landscape painters, but it was without doubt Edvard Munch, the father of expressionism, who with his clean and contrasting strokes, caught the restless, troubled and tormented soul. Spring, Girls on the Bridge and above all the Scream are his universal testimony.

Vigeland Sculpture Park: the bridge with bronze sculptures and the Monolith.

Young people in traditional costumes: Folk Museum in Oslo.

The authors Bjørnstjerne Bjørnson, the first Nobel laureate in literature, Jonas Lie and Knut Hamsun were some of those who wrote about the harsh living conditions of the country's peasantry and fishermen. But it was the playwright Henrik Ibsen who really knew how to convey the conflicts in society. With his work Peer Gynt, he created an image of the Norwegian soul, "To thine own self be true". In works such as In A Doll's House and Hedda Gabler, he becomes an early champion of women, and in An Enemy of the People, he shows the conflicts that arise between the individual and society.

Ibsen commissioned the Norwegian composer Edvard Grieg to write the score to Peer Gynt. Grieg made Norwegian folk music and parts of Norwegian history into universal classics. Grieg's music is known today in many parts of the world.

Celebrations, folk festivals and folklore

Norway's folk soul and traditions were created by hard work in barren nature, by the country's proud history and the oral literary and artistic traditions that existed in the heart of the people.

The red flag with the white and blue cross waves all over the country. The Norwegian people show their national pride through the flag, which is used for all occasions. The folk costume is an outfit many Norwegian women and men prefer when they really want to dress up for a special occasion, be it a wedding or various gala events. Each region has its own respective folk costume. There are both male and female costumes. The costumes that are mostly worn are those from Telemark and Hardanger. The various costumes can be seen in exhibitions at the Folk Museum in Oslo.

On National Day on May 17th, children and young people walk in a parade up Karl Johans Gate in Oslo towards the Palace to greet the royal family, while the people in the rest of the country celebrate the day in a traditional way. All of the country's traditions, ways of living and working, as well as old, typical houses have been well preserved in the various museums across the country. Folk museums and county museums are an important testimony of Norwegian culture. Many families use holidays and days off from work to visit the museums.

From when they are small, children learn to love their country, the people, the history and to protect nature.
Many traditions are kept alive in Norway, for example, folk dances from different parts of the country. These use instruments such as the langeleik, harmonica, and hardanger fiddle. The Sami have their own musical heritage based on joik and drums.
Wood has always been greatly used in Norway, obviously in housing but also in Norwegian crafts. Utensils such as plates and drinking cups are made from all types of wood. Woodcarving as an art form is highly appreciated. Art craftsmen have always been interested in figures from history and adventures. Fine copies of many ornaments and jewellery from the Viking era are also made. It is significant that Norway was among the first European countries that founded museums of design, with the museum that was opened in Oslo in 1876 being the first in Norway.

Historical dramatizations can be found in several places in Norway during the summer. The oldest and best known is the drama of Olav Haraldsson (the Holy) at the Battle of Stiklestad. Trolls are also part of fairy tales, small and large. They hide in the woods and turn up at night as "spirits", sometimes bad, sometimes mischievous, but they are always after something. In Oppdal and Heddal there are especially many fairy tales

Handicraft from the Viking era.

Troll.

The International Jazz Festival in Oslo.
Norway's National Day.

Holmenkollen.

Grieg. That is why, each year during the first week of August, a Peer Gynt Festival is held in Rondane.

Folk festivals in Scandinavia take place in connection with the different seasons. The main celebrations are held in the spring when light, snow melt and new life return. They culminate on June 23rd with the mid-summer and the Saint Hans celebration. This is the shortest night of the year and everyone gets together to chat, drink and dance, just as Munch's and Astrup's famous pictures show us.

Do not be surprised during your trip to Norway to discover a society that expresses its identity through history, adventure, music, dance and sports. Even in stores everything has a certain "traditional" feel, expressing a living soul, long hidden by a long period under a Danish and Swedish supremacy.

Therefore folk festivals, celebrations and sporting events are tinged with a nationalist echo to the beat of "Norway, Norway". Some of the most important celebrations are the Sami festivals, reindeer sled racing in Finnmark, the Birkebeiner sporting events, the Bergen International Festival, the North Cape March, the Viking Festival on Karmøy in Haugesund, the St. Olav festival, the Peer Gynt festival. A large number of music, theatre and film festivals are held across the country.

told about these creatures. Trolls, which children are often afraid of, are a depiction of human cruelty, stupidity and selfishness. Tourists often laugh of them because they are so ugly, but at the same time sympathetic and funny. You'll probably see them, and you can buy them as souvenirs of all sizes.

At Hunderfossen Family Park in Lillehammer, we get a glimpse into the world of trolls.

Recreation has deep historical roots in the country's history, legends and fairy tales. Even an historical figure such as Peer Gynt is almost an adventure hero and an example of the Norwegian folk soul thanks to the efforts of Ibsen and

Gastronomy

Norwegian food is tasty, varied and of very good quality. All the fish is first class. Herring and salmon are prepared in many different ways. Other common types of fish are trout, cod, pollock, mackerel, halibut, and whales, and an inexhaustible supply of shrimp. Norwegian cod is particularly good, often prepared in the oven and served with light sauces. All Scandinavians, including of course the Norwegians, are very fond of crayfish which are caught and eaten in august. There are also various gastronomic festivals held then that include this regal dish. Finally, we have to mention all the many different types of caviar: red, white, black, and served as a pâté. On the famous Fish Bryggen in Bergen, you can taste different types of offerings of fish as you walk between all the booths, or you can sit down and eat at one of the excellent restaurants close by if you prefer.

As for the meat dishes, we recommend those with reindeer meat that are typical of northern Norway, for example, ham and stew dishes with wild berries, which highlight the special flavour. In central and eastern Norway, elk and other wild game are dominant. One of the country's national dishes are meatballs, served with gravy and potatoes, often with sauerkraut and cranberries too. Grouse is a true delicacy. Norwegians prefer potatoes to both fish and meat. Other traditional dishes include porridge and pyttipanne, a tasty mixture of potatoes, vegetables and meat.

Norwegian cheeses are very good. In particular, Roquefort type cheeses may be mentioned, these are soft and

Shrimp.

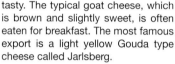

Smoked salmon.

Norwegian lamb stew.

tasty. The typical goat cheese, which is brown and slightly sweet, is often eaten for breakfast. The most famous export is a light yellow Gouda type cheese called Jarlsberg.

In Norway, people eat a lot of berries: raspberries, blueberries, cranberries and cloudberries are a popular dessert, both fresh and as an ingredient in cakes. Jam is also made from the berries which grow wild. Cloudberry Liqueur is an expensive delicacy. The most widespread type of berries are strawberries which are grown extensively. They and Norwegian apples are tasty, but there are also pears, morels and cherries. The raspberries that grow in northern Norway are pure delicacies, as are the waffles with whipped cream and blueberries

The water in Norway is very good, and milk, juice, tea or coffee is drunk at breakfast and other meals. Wine and champagne must be imported. All beers sold in Norway, both light beer and other types of beer are very tasty. We recommend trying a Hansa beer in Bergen, a Mack or Arctic in Tromsø and in Trondheim, a Lysholmer. In Oslo, Ringnes beer is sold.

Every visitor has to try the aquavit, which is made of potatoes and caraway, and in Norway is drunk with cured meats and sandwiches along with beer. Aquavit has an alcohol content of 45% to 54%, and has a particularly nice flavour. Aquavit is found throughout Scandinavia, and in Norway, Linje aquavit is one of the best.

One last recommendation: When in Finnmark, you should not miss a typical Sami meal, whether in a restaurant or in connection with a visit to one of the native "tribes" by the light of the midnight sun. A typical meal consists of Sami reindeer soup and reindeer stew with potatoes and cranberries. A very special menu which, in the company of the Lapps, their music and in their own environment, will give you a better understanding of this area far up north.

Famous Norwegians

Throughout the ages, many Norwegian citizens have made a great contribution to the country's political, social and cultural life. In politics we find new King Olav Tryggvason and Olav Haraldsson, known as Olav the Holy, and today as Harald V. Among politicians from recent times include Trygve Lie, who was the first Secretary General of the UN, and former Prime Minister Gro

Harlem Brundtland, who for several years was the Chief Executive of the World Health Organization.

In science, we can mention GH Armauer Hansen who discovered leprosy bacillus in 1874, and Kristian Birkeland, the first scientist who studied the Northern Lights. He is best known for the invention that made it possible to produce fertilizer from air.

Among the many explorers, sailors and other adventurers, we can mention the Vikings Erik the Red and his son Leif Eriksson, who discovered America in 1003; Fridtjof Nansen, Otto Sverdrup and Roald Amundsen, who explored the polar regions with the ships Gjoa and Fram and Thor Heyerdahl who crossed the Pacific Ocean and the Atlantic Ocean on rafts made of respectively balsa wood and papyrus.

It is quite natural that Norway's magnificent and beautiful scenery has influenced the work of its artists. In the visual arts, we can mention JCC Dahl and Edvard Munch, the father of expressionism. As a sculptor, Gustav Vigeland is unforgettable. In music, we must mention several, Edvard Grieg, Christian Sinding, Harald Sæverud and the composer and saxophonist Jan Garbarek as well as the trumpeter Ole Edvard Antonsen and the Sami singer Mari Boine.

Norway has ten Nobel Prize laureates, including three in literature: Bjørnstjerne Bjørnson (1903), Knut Hamsun (1920) and Sigrid Undset (1928). One must not forget plays such as those written by Henrik Ibsen, which revolutionized the European theatre in the last century. In film, it's actress and director Liv Ullmann who is the best known outside the country's borders

A country that is so cold in winter and has so many mountains must necessarily produce outstanding athletes. We want to mention Sondre Nordheim, who in 1870 set the standard for skiing and the figure skater Sonja Henie, who was the world champion for ten years in a row. In speed skating, and in a wide variety of sport skiing, we have a number of world champions.

Self-portrait by Edvard Munch. (Munch Museum)

Portrait of Henrik Ibsen, painted by Gustav J. Gulickson (Ibsen Museum).

Oslo seen from Oslofjorden.

1. EASTERN NORWAY: OSLO

Oslo, Viking Capital

The capital is situated at the head of Oslofjorden, 104 km inland from the Skagerrak, on the same latitude as St. Petersburg (Russia) and Anchorage (Alaska). It has an area of 454 km^2. Of these, 295 km^2 are forest land and 23 km^2 are parks. The city centre is located deep in the Nordmark, a beautiful forest area, which is a paradise for hiking in the summer, and a skier's winter's dream. This is perhaps one of the reasons the city was renamed Oslo, which means

"Gods grove" in the Viking language. Oslo has 620,000 inhabitants, 12% of the country's population. With the nature-filled surrounding suburbs, the population is around one million. Oslo is the capital of the Kingdom of Norway. The King's residence and Parliament are located here. The city also has a bishopric and universities. Oslo harbour has a 13 km long wharf. A large proportion of the country's imports and exports occurs here.

7000 years ago, when Oslo's first inhabitants settled by the bay, they lived in Ekebergåsen. A market arose in this fruitful and secure area. At

Akershus Fortress.

the head of the bay, where the old market stood, King Harald Hardrada founded the city around 1050. This location made it easy to control who came and went, especially the Danish military and traders. In 1299 King Håkon V moved the kingdom's capital from Bergen to Oslo, which had a safe harbour and a shorter way to the continent. To protect the capital, he built Akershus Fortress at the innermost part of the fjord. But the Hanseatic League, plagues, several fires and the union with Denmark made Oslo's development difficult.

In 1624 the city was destroyed by

another fire. Our union king Christian IV ordered that the city should be rebuilt at the Akershus Fortress, and named it Christiania, the name that the city retained until 1925.

The Centre's current lay-out stems from the beginning of the 1800s, when Norway was in a union with Sweden that began in 1814. In 1840 there were 20,000 residents in Christiania. The city was eventually built with Karl Johans Gate in the centre. The street went from the castle, built by the union king Karl Johan (in Sweden Carl XIV), to the train station. Important buildings like Parliament, the National Theatre and the University was built along Karl Johans Gate After the union with Sweden was dissolved in 1905, the construction of the Bergen Railway, which opened in 1909, and expansion of the port which meant a greater increase of shipping, Christiania became the country's major city. In 1925 it got back its old name, Oslo.

During World War II, from 1940 to 1945, Oslo was occupied by the Germans.

Post-war modern Oslo is marked by the Oslo City Hall, completed in 1950, on the occasion of the city's 900-year anniversary.

Today, after the discovery of oil in Norwegian territory in the 1970s, Oslo is a cosmopolitan city. The commercial and service industries flourish; you can go for a walk in one of the parks and visit interesting museums. One should not forget something so important internationally as the Nobel Peace Prize. The capital offers a wide range of festivals, but the most important is and remains the natural areas within the city limits - they make up 86% of Oslo's land mass.

In the centre: Karl Johans Gate, Oslo, Akerhus, the harbour and Aker Brygge

What is known as the centre of Oslo is situated between Karl Johans Gate, Akershus Fortress and Aker Brygge. Karl Johans Gate is the capital's main

The Palace on May 17th.

May 17th: the Norwegian Royal family greets the people who gather in front of the Palace.

Kofi Annan, Nobel Peace Prize winner 2001, greets people in Oslo from a balcony at the Grand Hotel.

street. It connects the castle with Central Station at Railway Square. Some of the city and the country's most prominent buildings are located along this street.

The **Royal Palace**, where the King performs many of his official duties, is located in **Slottspark**. The royal family stands on the palace balcony to greet the children when the parade passes by on National Day, May 17th. Tens of thousands of Norwegian children, many with the Norwegian flag painted on their face, greet the King while waving Norwegian flags. The Royal Palace was built by the union king Karl Johan. An equestrian statue of him stands in the Palace Square.

In Slottspark we can see a statue of Queen Maud, King Håkon VII's wife, who greets us as she stands in her spot among the trees.

On Drammensvei, across the street from one corner of the park, is the **Nobel Institute**, a yellow building in neoclassical style. In front stands the bust of the brilliant Swedish inventor Alfred Nobel. This is where the five members of the Nobel Committee each year discuss and submit their votes in order to crown the winner of the Nobel Peace Prize, which is awarded on December 10th, the anniversary of Alfred Nobel's death (1833-1896), in the City Hall reception hall. At the same time, the other Nobel Prizes are handed out in Stockholm. Ten Norwegians have received the Nobel Prize, including two Nobel Peace Prizes.

Further along Karl Johans Gate, towards the railway station, is the **National Theatre**, where, among other events, the Ibsen festival is held. In front of the building are

The National Theatre.

University of Oslo.

statues of Henrik Ibsen (1828-1906), our world-renowned playwright, and Bjørnstjerne Bjørnson (1832-1910), the first Nobel laureate in literature. Those who are particularly interested in Ibsen should visit the **Ibsen Museum**, which is located nearby, at 1 Arbins Street. The museum offers a guided tour through the house where he lived from 1895 until his death in 1906. Ibsen is perhaps the most universal of Norwegian writers. Above the National Theatre, on the other side of the street, are the oldest buildings which belong to the University of Oslo, founded in 1811. Today it is the country's largest university with approx. 40,000 students. This part of the university consists of three yellow coloured buildings in the classical style. Inside the building is the Aula, where many of the most important events in the history of Oslo are celebrated, and where the Nobel Peace Prize was awarded until 1990. The hall is decorated with Edvard Munch's outstanding murals. Behind the University, we find the **National**

The National Gallery.

Gallery, founded in 1836, which is Norway's largest art museum. The museum has, among other things, a very interesting collection of pictures by Edvard Munch, the father of expressionism. The collection consists of 58 works. Of these, we should highlight *The Scream, The Frieze of Life, The Girls on the Bridge, Spring* and *Self Portrait*. On the other side of Karl Johans gate, on Fridtjof Nansen plass, looms the majestic **Oslo City Hall**, which was completed in 1950 on the occasion of Oslo's 900-year anniversary. The City Hall consists of a main building with a large hall and several rooms used for public occasions, as well as two tall towers where the municipal administration has their offices. City Hall and the reception hall are adorned by the works of Norwegian artists. These tell the history from the olden days and up to when Norway was a free country after World War II. The Nobel Peace Prize is awarded each year on the December 10th, at a grand ceremony where the Royal Family is present.

Rådhuset (Oslo City Hall), Borggården.

Back on Karl Johans gate, we can see the park grounds in **Studenterlunden, Spikersuppa** and **Eidsvolls plass**. On this square is **Stortinget** (Parliament), built between 1861 and 1866, in the National Romantic style. **Stortinget** has 169 members, with a large number of women.

On the other side of Karl Johans gate, is the **Grand Hotel**. In earlier times,

Eidsvolls square with the Grand Hotel and Stortinget (Parliament).

Henrik Ibsen was one of the most famous regulars of the hotel's cafe. From Stortinget to the Central Station is the Karl Johan pedestrian street with shops, department stores, a market, pubs, street cafes, cafeterias, spontaneous performances, street musicians and people rushing in all directions. It is by far the liveliest district in the city while the shops are open and the weather is good. In the middle of this area is **Stortorvet**,

Interior of Stortinget.

The Norwegian Opera and Ballet.

an old square with a statue of King Christian IV. The Oslo Cathedral is also here. The cathedral was built in the 1600s, and was restored in 1950 and again in the early 2000's. It was here that Crown Prince Håkon Magnus married in 2001. The cathedral has an interesting altarpiece and pulpit from the late 1600's, as well as stained glass windows made by Emanuel Vigeland, brother of the famous sculptor.

Stortorvet.

Oslo Cathedral.

The Astrup Fearnley Museum.

Karl Johans gate ends at **Jernbanetorget** where the **Central Station** is. The **bus terminal** is also here as well as stations for the metro, trams, busses and trains. From here you can travel anywhere in Oslo, throughout the country and abroad.

In Oslo harbour there are always arrivals and departures of large ferries linking Oslo to Copenhagen, Gothenburg, Frederikshavn and Kiel. Always majestic and punctual. The ferries and the large cruise ships greet the capital in their magnificent way.

Akershus fortress and castle.

Christiania Torv: The Sculpture "Christian IV's Glove".

Oslo's premier historic neighbourhood is around **Akershus festning**, which Håkon V had built at the head of the bay when he moved the capital from Bergen, and which Christian IV had rebuilt in Danish Renaissance style in the 1600s.

Nowadays, large public receptions are held at Akershus. The fortress also contains the royal chapel and mausoleum. One of the finest things to do when visiting here is to walk on the ramparts and to take in the magnificent views of the bay, not to mention the **Hjemmefrontmuseet**, which shows what it was like for the Norwegian people during the war. One of the most interesting exhibits to visit is the story of the fight for heavy water in Telemark.

The view towards Akershus festning is the best from Aker Brygge. On the long and quiet Nordic nights, the calm sea shows off a sparkling and shining reflection of the fortress.

Nearby we find **old Christiania**, the oldest neighbourhood, with mansions and cobblestone streets, which was built on the orders of Christian IV after the fire of 1624. In this area there are several museums to choose from. One of the most interesting is the **Museum of Contemporary Art**, located at Bankplassen in the old premises of Norges Bank.

Aker Brygge has the city's best and liveliest nightlife.

In the period 1854-1982 parts of this area were a large shipyard, but in 1986 began the transformation into what we know today as Aker Brygge. In the 2000s Tjuvholmen grew as an extension of Aker Brygge.

The area is now known for its many restaurants and bustling life in the summer. But it also houses a large shopping mall, theatres, cinemas, offices, apartments and the newly opened Astrup Fearnley Museum, with its exciting new architecture.

Aker Brygge with Rådhuset.

Between Akershus and Aker Brygge is Rådhusplassen, a pedestrian paradise in the middle of Oslo, where one can admire the seaside from the city hall and a relief of St. Hallvard, the city's patron saint.

The Museums on Bygdøy

On the peninsula of Bygdøy, located approx. five kilometres from the city centre are several of Oslo's most interesting museums. The place is one of the most sought after residential areas, inhabited by politicians, artists and ambassadors. There are forests and idyllic beaches only a few minutes ride from the centre. The best way to get there is to take the ferry that runs from Rådhusplassen. The journey takes approx. 15 minutes. One can also take the number 30 bus from the city centre (Nationaltheatret) to Bygdøy.

Several of the museums here have to do with the sea and Norwegian history. The Viking Ship Museum, the Fram Museum, the Kon-Tiki Museum and the Norwegian Maritime Museum. Visiting these four interesting museums is the best way to learn about the Norwegians' many and dramatic adventures on the seven seas.

Another major museum on Bygdøy is the **Norwegian Folk Museum**. Here you can walk in the open air between old houses and buildings from all over Norway. We can mention in particular the stave church from Gol, a street with old buildings from Christiania, and halls with interesting exhibits of traditional costumes and Sami culture. At the museum you can also see displays of folk dancing and other types of outdoor activities.

Close by is the **Vikingskipshuset**, which contains the world's best preserved Viking ship. The

Norwegian Folk Museum.

archaeological cultural heritage of the Norwegian Vikings is divided between the History Museum, located in the city behind the National Gallery, and this museum. But one can arguably say that the most interesting objects are here, in this *temple*, shaped almost like a church, to emphasize its great value. The museum was built between 1926 and 1932, as a project of Arnstein Arneberg, one of the architects of City Hall.

The building consists of five sections. In the main hall, you'll find the Oseberg ship. This is the best preserved of all the ships. The ship was built ca. AD 800, and discovered in 1904. It is believed that it was the grave of the Viking Queen Åsa, who was buried with a maid and all her belongings. To the left is the Gokstad ship from ca. 875, discovered in 1880, a drake (warship) which is more streamlined, but strong and secure. It was with this

The Oseberg ship at Vikingskiphuset.

type of ship that Vikings ventured out on the ocean.

To the right we find the remains of the Tune ship. This was discovered in 1867. It has not been possible to restore the ship, but we can clearly see the solid and secure way the Vikings built their ships.

At the back of the building all the various objects that were found in the vessels are on display. Wooden sleds, a cart, fabrics, shoes, pots, utensils, chests, etc. In short, all it takes for us to imagine how the Vikings lived.

You should not miss the small but important exhibit on the second floor. It shows the Vikings' travel and cruises, an interesting model of a settlement, and a case with copies of objects that were found in Anse-Aux-Meadows in Newfoundland in Canada. There are simple objects such as a needle, a lamp and ballast materials, but there is clear evidence that the Vikings were in North America 500 years before Columbus. Next, we come to the tip of the peninsula where there are three very interesting museums: the Norwegian Maritime Museum, the Fram Museum and the Kon-Tiki Museum.

Norwegian Maritime Museum contains a collection of model ships covering the entire Norwegian seafaring history from primitive fishing boats to large whaling ships. The museum also has a Super Panorama Cinema, a theatre with five screens, where an impressive film by Ivo Caprino about the Norwegian coast is shown. There is also a restaurant. Outside the museum is a kiosk that serves coffee and light meals as well as a terrace with a breathtaking view of the bay and Oslo.

The Fram museum is an example of very special architecture, and here you can explore the polar ship Fram. It was built by Colin Archer in Larvik in 1892, for Fridtjof Nansen's (1861-1930) first expedition to the North Pole. Otto Sverdrup - who later created the museum - led the four-year expedition around Greenland that began in 1898. In 1910-11 Roald Amundsen (1872-1928) used the ship on his expedition to the South Pole. The museum also contains maps and

Norwegian Maritime Museum, Fram Museum and the Kon-Tiki Museum.

outstanding photographs showing how challenging and dramatic the expeditions of Nansen, Sverdrup and Amundsen were.

The **Kon-Tiki** Museum displays the latest addition about the intense relationship between Norwegians and the sea. The museum tells us about the travels of the explorer Thor Heyerdahl (1914-2002). Heyerdahl wanted to prove by his travels that there was a connection between the great primitive cultures. Here you can learn about all his expeditions. Not the least about the raft Kon-Tiki, which he rode from Peru to Polynesia, and the raft RA II, on which he managed to cross the Atlantic Ocean, from Morocco to Barbados. The museum has a display of an overview of Heyerdahl's expeditions: Fatu-Hiva, Galapagos, Easter Island, etc. There is a small cinema that shows movies about the travels of Thor Heyerdahl. We especially recommend the film of the Kon-Tiki expedition. Even without words, it is easy to understand that this was a brilliant project and a genius of a man.

And now back to Oslo. On the way to the pier where we take the boat to Rådhusplassen, we pass **the schooner Gjøa**. Roald Amundsen sailed on it for the first time through the Bering Strait.

Kon-Tiki.

The Fram Museum and the Fram.

Vigeland Sculpture Park: "The Source and The Tree of Life" and "The Angry Boy".

Vigeland Sculpture Park and the Munch Museum

Two cultural institutions are a must-see in Oslo are the Vigeland Sculpture Park, or Frognerparken, as it's also called, and the Munch Museum.

Frognerparken is a large park of 320,000 square metres, the largest green space in the middle of town. Many of Oslo's residents use the park in summer and winter to stroll, jog, play tennis, swim or simply relax and soak up the sun as soon as it comes out. Inside the park you can admire a collection of sculptures that are so impressive that it has led to the park now being more commonly known as the Vigeland Sculpture Park.

Gustav Vigeland (1869-1943) learned the art of stone carving under the influence of world classics and the Dane Bissen. In 1921, he gave all his future work to the city of Oslo, in exchange for the authorities to build him a studio/private residence and to give him a large park where he could exhibit most of his sculptures. Vigeland worked on the sculptures in the park for almost twenty years. He made 212 groups in bronze, iron and granite, but died before everything was completed.

Vigeland never explained if his sculptures had a special message. But as you can see they can have a thousand different interpretations and represent a magnificent reproduction of human life. Greatness, emotions and conflicts are presented in a wonderful way for the joy and inspiration of future generations.

The main entrance to the park has beautiful wrought iron gates designed by the artist himself. The park shows us the cycle of life, from birth, to youth and old age. Vigeland also worked with the theme "The Source of Water and the Tree of Life" - a large fountain that is held by six atlases, provides water for life, nature and people. On the "Tree of Life" hang children, adolescents, fathers and mothers, the old and the dead. This cycle of life is repeated in the friezes at the bottom of the fountain.

On the stairs towards the Monolith are 36 groups carved in granite. These reflect the different stages of life. The Monolith is almost 18 metres high and consists of 121 characters dramatically entwined about each other until they reach the top, which is conquered by a child. This part of the park ends with a sundial, which shows the horoscope and symbolizes time, and a wheel with seven intertwining bodies where life and death - the beginning and the end - complete the circle.

All the sculptures, which are very large, are magnificent in their expressiveness and drama.

Those who want to know more about Vigeland and his work can visit his workshop, which is now a museum – **the Vigeland Museum**. Here you can see the drawings, models, projects, models for the sculptures and the whole story behind the creation of the park.

The Vigeland Museum.

Munch Museum. Exterior and the painting "The Voice 1893".

Edvard Munch (1863-1944) is one of Scandinavia's greatest painters, and his work addresses some of the major themes in art from the late 1800's and early 1900's. The anxiety of life, loneliness, fear and death. These themes and his trademark style made Munch the father of expressionism. His strong, violent and occasionally large colour contrasts and brush strokes, show us the power that he possessed.

During his childhood he was deeply affected by the death of his mother, sister and brother, but his artistic life was very stimulating. Munch's work frequently returns to illness, death and grief, themes that are often present in his pictures. Therefore, they make us feel anxious more often than they make us feel satisfied Munch's pictures are a balance of landscapes of the fatherland, sometimes realistic, sometimes symbolically dramatic - and the melancholy interiors of illness and death in a weak, Nordic light. Family members and friends are other protagonists who ask us about the meaning of life from pictures like *Four Girls in Åsgårdstrand* to *The Sick Child* and the world-famous *The Scream*, of which he painted several versions.

The Munch Museum opened in 1963. It contains more than 1100 paintings, 4700 drawings and 18,500 lithographs. A walk through the modern halls gives a special insight into the country and the soul of the artist.

This visit can be combined with a walk in the nearby **Botanical gardens**, or you can take advantage of the excellent facilities at **Tøyenbadet**, to swim, sunbathe or take a relaxing sauna.

Oslo's surroundings

Oslo's surroundings provide an intense first contact with the Norwegian countryside. It's full of surprises, breathtaking scenery, incredible scenery, interesting buildings and very interesting museums. A unique blend of nature and culture.

Holmenkollbakken is situated 417 metres above sea level. It was built in 1892 and has since been rebuilt several times, in keeping with the development of the sport of skiing. The current Holmenkollbakke was built new for the FIS World Cup in 2010. You can get to it by train from the city centre, but we recommend driving and enjoying the view from the road that winds its way up through one of the most beautiful residential areas not only in Oslo, but in all of Scandinavia. You can drive the car right up to the ski jump and see the city from the stands. You take the lift up to the top of the tower which is 60 metres above the ground where the view of Oslo and the fjord are just fantastic. Then you can see how this city, like so many others in Scandinavia, is surrounded by nature. We must not forget that Oslo means "Gods grove".

Ever since 1892, world championships in ski jumping have been held at Holmenkollbakken. On Holmenkoll Day in March, thousands of Norwegians come here, many of them on foot, in order to attend of the winter's most popular ski festivals.

Next to the jump is the Ski Museum which contains, among other things, one of Norway's oldest skis, found in Alvdal, as well as equipment, materials and clothing from the expeditions of Nansen and Amundsen. A new and larger Ski Museum was built for the Nordic World Ski Championships in 2011.

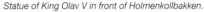

Statue of King Olav V in front of Holmenkollbakken.

Holmenkollen.

Holmenkollen is a popular destination for Oslo's residents. Here they go hiking in summer and skiing in winter. Can you imagine going straight from work, taking the train, putting on your skis and then skiing back to town? Few capitals can offer anything like it. Do not forget to pay a visit to the **Holmenkollen Park Hotel Rica** which is 200 metres to the right below the ski jump. It is a beautiful building in the so-called Dragon style that originated in Norway around the turn of the century, with red-painted wooden walls, sloping ceilings and decoration in the style of stave churches and the newly excavated Viking ships. One of the few and precious examples of this architectural style that are to be found in the country.

A few miles above Holmenkollen is **Tryvannstårnet**, which is 118 metres high. Up here, the air is always clean and fresh. In this sea of green trees, there are numerous trails and roads where you can ski in the winter and hike in the summer. You can also take a refreshing dip in one of the many lakes - Oslo has 343 lakes within the city limits.

Another interesting option is a cruise on Oslofjorden. Oslofjorden runs into the Skagerrak, and is 104 km long, half as long as the Sognefjord, the world's longest fjord. It has two branches, but just the western branch exits to the open sea. The mainland, islands, reefs, coves, beaches, forests, fields and the sea's wildlife, have provided for an idyllic setting, food and wealth to the people who have lived on the shores of Oslofjorden, including the capital's inhabitants.

Inside one of the fjords is the **Henie Onstad Art Centre**, opened in 1968 by the famous figure skater, Olympic champion and film actress Sonja Henie and her husband, shipping magnate Niels Onstad. It is the largest centre for contemporary art (figurative art, theatre, film, music, dance, etc.), the Centre's collections of styles such as cubism, surrealism and abstract art are particularly interesting.

If you are travelling with children perhaps the best choice is **Tusenfryd**, a "modern" amusement park. The park is located outside the city.

Tryvann Tower.

Oslo and the fjord seen from Hovedøya.

Drøbak and Oscarsborg.

Moss, Halden and Fredrikstad:
the Old Town.

The East Coast of Oslofjorden

A pleasant and enjoyable outing is to drive on E6 from Oslo towards the Swedish border along the east coast of Oslofjorden. On the way to the border are the towns and villages of **Drøbak, Moss, Fredrikstad, Sarpsborg** and **Halden**. Drøbak is a beautiful little town with an ancient harbour and typical, white-painted wooden houses; Moss is a somewhat larger city. Fredrikstad is currently the only fully preserved fortress in Scandinavia (founded in 1567) and has witnessed many battles between Norwegian, Danish and Swedish forces. In Halden, just two kilometres from the Swedish border, is the imposing fortress Fredriksten, which was built in the 1600's.

Kragerø.

2. SOUTH NORWAY

South Norway does not have Western Norway's stunning scenery with deep fjords and high mountains, or Northern Norway's endless plains. Here nature is ever changing. From the coast, the beaches and the small beach towns, Skagerrak and the many bays and islands in Oslofjorden, the narrow valleys in Setesdal and the mountains, forests and open land with vast plains of Telemark. E18 runs south from Oslo along the shore, past beaches, hills and villages that in the summer are full of tourists. South Norway is also known as Norway's "Riviera" and "route through the white towns".

Risør.

Lyngør.

Arendal: City Hall and the harbour.

After driving a way, we come to **Åsgårdstrand**. Here you will find Munch's house which is now a museum. Munch painted many pictures here, including the famous *Girls on the Bridge*.

After that comes Tønsberg, Norway's oldest city, founded as early as 871 In the next town of **Sandefjord**, which in its time was a centre of the whaling industry, is the interesting Whaling Museum.

A few kilometres further south take the road to Skien, the main town in Telemark (see itinerary 3).

We follow the coast south and drive past **Kragerø, Risør, Tvedestrand, Arendal** and **Grimstad**. These towns are popular holiday destinations during the summer, with their whitewashed wooden houses, narrow streets, cosy marinas and white sandy beaches. It hosts both festivals and

Arendal: Tromøya.

Grimstad.

Lillesand.

Kristiansand.

other cultural events. The Wooden Boat Festival in Risør is a very special event. When we walk along the streets of these cities, we understand why Munch chose many of these places as the ideal setting for his pictures.

In **Grimstad**, we find the Ibsen Museum in the pharmacy where the author worked from 1844 to 1850. Here is where he wrote his first play.

Before we get to Kristiansand, we can visit **Lillesand**, which is also a popular summer holiday destination. The city has a nice harbour surrounded by beautiful houses, where the famous Town Hall is also located.

Kristiansand, 320 km south of Oslo, is the capital of South Norway. It is an important industrial city and the gateway to the country for Danes, Germans and Englishmen who come by ferry from Hirtshals on the other side of the Skagerrak.

The city is Norway's fifth largest with 83,000 inhabitants, and is the administrative centre for the Vest-Agder. Kristiansand was founded in 1641 by King Christian IV. The city has preserved an old part of the centre in the Renaissance style. Here you find the cathedral and the city hall and the ever lively Markens gate. Along all the straight alleyways, we can admire the many beautiful houses from the 1700s, and by the beach, we find the city' castle. Here there is also a statue of Henrik Wergeland, one of Norway's greatest poets, who was born here. The statue is one of Gustav Vigeland's most famous work.

We want to mention in particular the open-air museum Vest-Agder Museum and the Cannon Museum with the world's second largest cannon with 38 cm caliber, which can

Kristiansand: The shopping street.

Kristiansand: from the harbour and the city beach.

Kristiansand: The market place and the cathedral.

Mandal.

Sjøsanden, Mandal.

Lindesnes lighthouse.

shoot halfway to the Danish coast. Last but not least, Norway's largest zoological park, Kristiansand Zoo with Torbjørn Egner Cardamom Town and Kaptein Sabeltanns (Captain Sabertooth's) world.

We continue south and come to **Mandal**, the country's southernmost city, where there are also many typical, white-painted wooden houses. Gustav Vigeland was born here. In Mandal you will also find Sjøsanden beach, one of the largest and most famous in all of southern Norway.

We continue past the deserted coasts, rocks and mountains, to **Lindesnes**. This is Norway's southernmost point, which is lies at 58° north out into the North Sea. A lighthouse surrounded by breathtaking scenery, windy, rocky coasts, reefs, fjords and open sea, and a sign welcoming you to Norway. The sign informs us that it is 1.752 km to the North Cape, at 71° north.

Fedafjord.

We continue to the beautiful **Fedafjorden**, where the town of **Flekkefjord** is located. Here we visit the interesting and cosy Hollenderbyen with county estates from the 17th and 18th centuries, built by Dutchmen who settled here.

Right after that, we come to Rogaland County and are now in the western part of the country and the fjords of Norway

Flekkefjord.

Evje, Setesdal.

3. SOUTH NORWAY: SETESDAL AND TELEMARK

Setesdalen is one of the most interesting areas in southern Norway. Because of its isolated location, the valley not only has preserved nature, but also its way of living, traditions and language. The valley is an outstanding example of the peasant culture that has now more or less vanished.

It is a relatively narrow valley where the river Otra winds downwards. It extends from Haukeligrend in northwestern Telemark to Kristiansand on the coast. The journey through the valley is 240 km, on a winding, shifting road, full of surprises. Here we can admire the beautiful scenery along the river Otra. Water and waterfalls, forests and mountains, villages and farms, all of which give the valley a typical Norwegian appearance, rooted in the past.

From Kristiansand, you can take the museum train **Setesdalsbanen** to the southern part of the valley. It is a train with wooden carriages pulled by a steam locomotive from 1901. In the past it went to Byglandsfjorden, today only the first kilometres to Grovane are left.

On the way up, we drive past **Mushom**, the mining area **Hornnes**, and the interesting Setesdal Mineral Park, which has 175 metres of mine paths and entrances to some of the mines in the area. In this area, we can sometimes see Setesdal's typical octagonal churches and farms with many houses, where you primarily notice storehouses. They are all made of solid timber that resists the ravages of time.

After **Evje** we come to **Byglandsfjorden**, where the river forms two lakes that often show off beautiful reflections of the surroundings. There are good conditions for fishing and many water sports. Farther north in the towns of **Helle, Hylestad** and **Nomeland** craftsmen are specialized in making traditional silver jewellery.

In Nomeland we can drive over to the West Coast on a winding road that leads to Lysebotn and Lysefjord. The road passes through magnificent mountain scenery and is probably the most spectacular road in southern Norway. On the way to the Lysefjord is a descent of 932 metres with 27 turns. It is an experience that can only be compared to Trollstigen in Møre og Romsdal.

We continue our journey towards **Valle** and **Setesdalsmuseet**, where we can admire an interesting collection of buildings from the 1500's and an outstanding view of the traditions of Setesdal. Just before Rygnestad begins County Road 45, which takes us to Telemark.

Telemark County stretches from the shores of Oslofjorden, the county's largest twin city of Skien/Porsgrunn, to **Gaustatoppen** (1883m), which is the centre of a mountain area with forests, rivers, lakes and mountains with eternal snow. Just like Setesdal, Telemark has also preserved its nature, which is always green with a prominent blue tinge, and its habitat. Here we can admire the traditional buildings with beautiful decorative painting, porches adorned with flowers - and storehouses. The county has also maintained its folklore, dialect, crafts and typical costumes displayed with pride everywhere throughout the county, especially during the Telemark Festival in Bø.

Telemark is also known all over the world, thanks to two events. Here we find the cradle of skiing, in Morgedal. Vemork/Rjukan and the battle for heavy water are well known from the Second World War.

Skiing was born in Telemark. Not as a sport, but as a result of a need related to the environment and lifestyle. It was Sondre Nordheim (1825-1897) from Morgedal who "invented" modern

The Setesdal Museum in Valle.

Krossobanen cable car up to Gvepseborg. In the background: Gaustatoppen.

Norwegian Industrial Workers Museum.

skiing. At ski exhibition in Oslo in 1868, he presented a revolutionary technique - the curved ski - which meant that it was much easier to manoeuvre the skis. Norway is the country of origin of the expression and skiing technique known as the "telemark turn" and "slalom", which in the local dialect means "downhill slope". Today there is a centre for modern skiing in **Morgedal**, the cradle of skiing, which, among other things, contains a replica of Sondre Nordheim's home.

The only place in Norway where heavy water was able to be produced during the war, the main component that was necessary to make a nuclear bomb, were the Norsk Hydro plants at Vemork near **Rjukan**. The Germans began to produce heavy water here. After the Allies had conducted a failed sabotage attempt, they carried out a bombing raid which unfortunately resulted in significant civilian casualties. But finally the home front's resistance managed to sink the

Kongsberg.

ferry that transported the remaining heavy water to its final destination in Germany. The French-Norwegian film production "The Battle for Heavy Water" (1948), by Titus Vibe-Müller and Jean Dreville, and the American film "The Heroes of Telemark" by Anthony Mann, both tell the story. These achievements are discussed at the **Industrial Workers Museum at Vemork**, where you can also see other exhibitions on industrial workers' working conditions, mines and industrial development in Norway. If we take County Road 45 from Setesdal, we can take the exit to Morgedal on the right, and to Rjukan on the left. In Rjukan there is a cable car that ascends to 890 metres above sea level to Gvepseborg. From Rjukan, there's a path that leads up to Gaustatoppen. It takes around three hours to get there. From the top there is a spectacular view of the mountains. We continue to **Kongsberg** located at

Numedalslågen. This is a mining and industrial city that is also a popular ski resort. The city currently has 25,500 inhabitants, but in the 1700's it was Norway's second largest city (after Bergen) thanks to silver mining. Here we can visit the unique church in a Baroque and Rococo style that was inaugurated in 1761, and the Mining Museum, which together with the Ski Museum, Kongsberg Arms Factory Museum and the Royal Mint Museum, are housed in the old smelter.

The mines in **Saggrenda** are also interesting. They have a depth of up to 1070 metres and you can ride a small train through three kilometres of mine paths.

About 30 miles west of the road E134 is **Notodden** and **Heddal** church, the largest of the preserved wooden churches from the Middle Ages. Due to the size it is known as "Stavkirke cathedral". It was built around 1150, expanded in 1250, and has a unique

Notodden.

Heddal Stave Church.

decor with dragons, animals and flowers. The church was restored in 1954.

At **Heddal Farm** we can see one of the most beautiful examples of decorated houses in Telemark, painted by Olav Hansson. Two of the motifs that recur in the decoration of the building are roses and acanthus leaves. The tradition of rose painted houses, walls and household objects became fashionable in the 1700's. That is when people started putting in windows and chimneys to ventilate their houses, so that soot would no longer damaged the paint.

On Notodden we can experience another of the county's interesting features, namely the Telemark Canal. It was opened in 1892 and is 110 km long. One part goes north from Skien to Notodden and Heddal, and another west to the valley. You can take an adventurous boat ride that goes through 18 locks, all operated by hand. During the trip you can enjoy the landscape and natural contrasts of farmland, lush vegetation, lakes and mountains.

In **Bø**, on the way to Skien, is the water park **Bø Summerland**. The park has generators that create waves so you can go surfing

In **Skien**, located on the shores of the Telemark Canal, we recommend paying a visit to Ibsen's house, which is now an important cultural centre as well as Brekkeparken, a museum with interesting exhibits that show how the bourgeoisie lived in the 1700's.

Telemark Canal.

Before we leave, we must mention the Telemark village of **Fyresdal** with its beautiful scenery and the Fyresdal museum which has a nice exhibit of the traditions of the area. We must not forget Haukeliveien which begins in Haukeligrend. The road was opened in 1896 and reaches a height of 1133 m.

Driving this road is a wonderful nature experience, you can admire the beautiful valleys, rivers and waterfalls near the glaciers.

Skien.

Prekestolen in Lysefjord.

4. WESTERN NORWAY:
FROM STAVANGER TO BERGEN

Fjord-Norway

The fjords are Norway's best known natural feature. To understand how they came into being, we must go far back in time, when the Scandinavian Peninsula was covered by ice that melted gradually as the temperature rose. The inland ice covering Scandinavia was several kilometres thick and pressed masses of land down into the earth. When the ice melted around 10,000 years ago, the land and the sea penetrated into the valleys which the ice had formed on its way to the sea. Thus the fjords. A fjord is therefore either a U-shaped glacier valley or a V-shaped valley, where the bottom is formed by the water from the melting ice that has flown down to the bottom of the ice mass. Fjords appear as deep sea passages that enter into the land. All fjords have a main branch and smaller side branches. The entire Norwegian coast is like this, from Oslo in the south to Finnmark in the north, with islands, reefs, islets, steep mountain sides and many fjord branches that cut into the land.

It is without a doubt the fjords of western Norway that are the most spectacular. Here we can experience one of the most beautiful and intense scenes of nature. The fjord landscape is incredibly beautiful. It impresses in a way that cannot be described.

Stavanger

We begin our journey on the west coast in the south. Rogaland has an area of over 9,000 km^2, with a population of 443,000 and is the county with the greatest number of companies related to the oil industry in the country. We can take E18 from Oslo onto E39 from Kristiansand, or E134 from Bergen. The county is 450 km from Oslo, has two airports, one in Stavanger and one in Haugesund, as well as excellent boat connections with Denmark.

Stavanger is the county's largest city and the fourth largest in Norway with 128,000 residents. A large town or a small city - but very vibrant and international, thanks to all the activity going on in connection with oil and gas development in the North Sea.

We begin our walking tour of the city by visiting the old city centre. In "**Old Stavanger**", with its cobbled streets, you can admire over 170 houses from the 1700's and 1800's, most of which are painted white. Stavanger has

Norway's oldest **cathedral** (built in the 1100's in the Romanesque style). The city centre surrounds **Breiavatnet**, where we find shops, cafes, historic buildings and a park that give the "oil capital" a welcoming, open and cosmopolitan feel. The picturesque harbour area should also be visited.

If you want to walk in history's footsteps, Stavanger is proud to show it to you at its three museums: the **Maritime Museum**, the **Canning Museum**, as well as the **Norwegian Petroleum Museum**.

But if you want to know where some of the most important pages in the city's history were written, you should go outside the city to **Hafrsfjord**, where Harald Fairhair won the battle that turned Norway into a single kingdom in 872. The monument **Swords in the mountain**, which are three giant

Stavanger seen from the air.

swords plunged into the mountain, was erected to commemorate this historic event as a visual symbol of this region's Viking past.

Another key testament from the Norwegian Middle Ages is the Augustine monastery **Utstein Kloster**, set out in the archipelago. It was built in the 1200's and is possibly the best preserved medieval monastery in the country.

From Stavanger to Bergen

As we continue on from Stavanger we can enjoy still more examples of the beautiful Norwegian nature. Not far from the city, we find the county's

most visited attraction, **Lysefjord** with the famous **Pulpit Rock**, a cliff with a vertical drop of 604 metres that hangs out over the fjord. From Stavanger boat excursions are arranged to Lysefjord.

The fjord is narrow, U-shaped and about 45 km long. There is lush scenery and impressive cliffs around it that run vertically down the fjord which here has an intense green colour. One might say that the Pulpit rock is Rogaland's top tourist attraction. Excursions there are almost always by boat. These sail past the beautiful island landscape of

Stavanger harbour.

The monument "Swords in Rock" in Hafrsfjord.

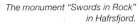

Stavanger Cathedral and Old Stavanger.

Kjerrag in Lysefjorden.

Ryfylke, and into the fjord at the foot of Pulpit rock. On a clear day, the view from the top is fantastic.

Some of the excursions end with a bus journey back to Stavanger, so that one can see the interior of Rogaland. **Haugesund**, which has approx. 35,000 inhabitants, has a nice harbour which is nice for taking a walk. Outside the town is Haraldshaugen, dedicated to the memory of Harald Fairhair and the unification of the country. It was built where it is believed that this legendary Viking king is buried. It is a monolith surrounded by 29 smaller standing stones representing the 29 chiefs Harald had to overcome in order to unify Norway under one king.

The historic site, Avaldsnes, is worth a visit.

We are now on E-134 and coming into **Hordaland County**. Hordaland has an area of 15.634 km² and 491,000 inhabitants. Of those, a little over half reside in Bergen. In Hordaland the landscape becomes more open and wider, particularly at **Hardangerfjord**, which with its 179 km² is Norway's third longest fjord. Here we see the rivers, lakes, waterfalls and numerous rock outcrops that hang out over the fjord.

At **Jøsendal** we take County Road 13 that runs along **Sørfjorden**, the fjord's southern branch. On this trip we find two towns, **Odda** and **Lofthus**, the latter was one of Edvard Grieg's favourite places, and **Låtefossen**, a twin waterfall that is one of our most spectacular waterfalls, especially when the ice melts in the spring. If you are in Odda, take Motorway 550 to Eitrheim. Here you turn left, drive through the Folgefonn tunnel to Gjerde, and follow Motorway 48 to Rosendal. This is the country's only barony. The main building was erected in 1665 by Ludvig Rosenkrantz. It is not just the Barony, but also concerts, plays and exhibitions which each year attract many tourists to the place.

East of this area is the **Hardangervidda National Park**, covering an area of 3.422 km². We can still see herds of caribou. It is a large mountain plateau that is between 1,100 and 1,400 metres high, with a lack of vegetation reminiscent of northern Norway. The plateau is covered by snow and ice most of the year. In summer it is covered with moss, grass and brush. It's a nice place to go hiking, and if you are lucky you can see large caribou herds in the distance. It is also recommended to try your luck at fishing in one of the plateau's many basins and lakes. At the side of the road, inside the national park, there is a small Sami settlement with houses of sod, a siida (summer

Haraldshaugen National Monumnet.

camp) and souvenir sales. When we drive out of the park and begin the descent to Hardangerfjorden, we find **Vøringsfossen**. With a drop of 182 metres, it is one of the highest in Norway and one of the most impressive. We recommend stopping at the Fossli hotel and admire the falls from the hotel terrace.

Lofthus.

Låtefoss.

We drive down Måbødalen and come to **Eidfjord**, the innermost of Hardangerfjorden's branches. A short drive brings us to **Brimnes**, where a brief but exciting crossing by ferry brings us to **Bruravik**. If you stand on the deck, the natural experience is even stronger, while being accompanied by wind and cries of the seagulls. When we drive off the ferry, a narrow road leads us to Ulvik, one of the loveliest spots on the fjord. This is the gem of Hardanger, a small village at the head of Ulvikfjorden. Here you can combine the peace and quiet with several different activities. A fascinating flight over the fjord and the deep, narrow valleys. There are tours of the nearby glaciers, boating, other water sports, or bird watching in the woods.

Driving to Bergen, we recommend taking Motorway 7 which runs along the northern shore of Hardangerfjorden. Thanks to its fine microclimate, this fjord has many residents. It also has plenty to offer to tourists. The best season to visit Hardangerfjorden is in the spring when the shores of the fjord are full of blossoming fruit trees. The snow-capped mountains are reflected in the fjord and the sky is an intense and pure blue colour. The residents are proud of their home because nowhere else in the country can you find similar display of Norwegian folklore. Here we can enjoy fiddling, traditional costumes with beautiful silver jewellery, wedding dresses with crowns, wooden handicrafts, and not to forget the big beer mugs which are reminiscent of the Vikings, as well as wedding celebrations, folk festivals and dancing. The area around the fjord is the place in Norway where traditional Norwegian culture has been best preserved, and Edvard Grieg has spread it throughout the world with his wonderful music. The road runs along the bay past the towns of **Øystese**, home of "the eternal deuce", sculptor Ingebrigt Vik and his small, but impressive museum and **Norheimsund**. In the latter is Steinsdalsfossen, an impressive waterfall where you can walk *under* the waterfall.

Vøringsfoss.

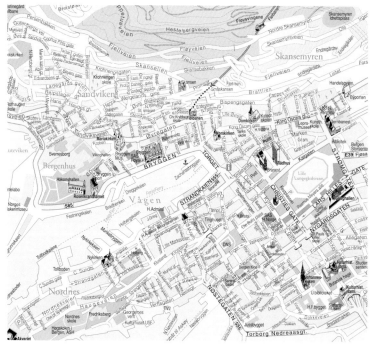

Bergen.

5. WESTERN NORWAY: BERGEN, THE CAPITAL OF FJORD-NORWAY

There are many myths and facts that describe Norway's second largest city and the country's former capital. That it is the biggest hanseatic port and Norway's music capital, Edvard Grieg's home, Norway's most picturesque city, the city where it never stops raining and the city that has the best salmon. The city is host to many seminars, conferences and festivals. All visitors love this city because of its scenery, monuments and environment. Bergen is also the city with the most calls by cruise ships and is the country's main hub for tourist traffic. Of the many attractions, we want to mention the fish market on Torget, Grieg's home Troldhaugen and the cable train Fløibanen.

Bergen is an impressive sight as it is surrounded by seven mountains, with houses painted in many colours that lie in a series of rows at the foot of the mountains. The ground, lakes and islands form a multicoloured jigsaw puzzle with the North Sea as a backdrop: a unique fusion of nature and buildings. To really enjoy this first impression, you can either take the cable train up to **Fløien**, which is 320 metres above sea level in the middle of the city near the harbour. From there you have a wonderful view of the city centre. Or you can take the cable car up to Ulriken, which is 600 metres above sea level. From here there are magnificent views of Bergen and the surroundings, the mountains, the fjord and ocean. If you have time, we recommend this last option. Bergen has 265,000 inhabitants and is the "gateway" to the fjord- Norway. It is an administrative city, the nation's second-largest university and an important industrial city. A haven of great activity, fishing and starting point for **Hurtigruten** (Express ship route), which runs all the way to Finnmark.

Bergen is also the capital of arts and culture. Here we find the National Theatre and the Bergen International

Funicular railway "Fløibanen" and Bergen.

Bergen seen from Ulriken.

Bergen seen from the air.

Festival. The city also hosts many other festivals, conferences and congresses. The city was one of the European "Capitals of Culture" in 2000.

While the city is cosmopolitan and full of life, Bergen has managed to preserve its history and rich heritage. The city was founded in 1070 by King Olav Kyrre and was Norway's capital for over 200 years. Because of its great location the harbour soon became the basis for the port city's economic development. The development was mainly based on the dried and salted fish trade, especially cod, which came from the major fishing grounds along the coast. Lofoten fishery was by far the most important.

Beginning in the mid-1300s Bergen became a hanseatic city. German merchants, in particular those from Lubeck, turned the city's port into the North Sea's most important centre for receiving and exporting fish. The vessels came into Bergen fully loaded with cod from Lofoten, which after being processed and preserved, was reloaded and taken south to the ports of the Baltic and North Germany. From there, they found their way especially to Catholic countries. Fish was an important and necessary food during Lent. The hanseatic section of the city with its houses, streets, gathering places and strict rules, worked as a small, strict German world until 1754, when "The Office" was shut down. Cod laid the foundation for the city's prosperity.

Modern Bergen began to develop in the early 1900's. First, there was the construction of the Bergen Railway, which was completed in 1909. This is the railway that daily connects the country's two largest cities. After the great fire of 1916, which laid the city centre in ashes and a new city was created. During World War II the

5. Western Norway: Bergen, The Capital of Fjord-Norway

Bergen: Torgalmenningen.

Vågen in Bergen.

Bryggen.

city was occupied by the Germans, who turned the port into its main submarine base for the North Sea and Atlantic Ocean. In 1944 a ship loaded with explosives blew up in the harbour and destroyed parts of the old city centre.

Today the most important historic buildings have been rebuilt.

The town centre surrounds the

From the Hanseatic Museum.

Maria Church

Part of Grieg's genius was to use Norwegian folk music, especially from Hardanger. He turned folk music to classical music and in that way made it universal. Grieg's music brings to our imaginations the adventures and legends of the great Norwegian folk heroes like Sigurd the Crusader and Olaf Tryggvason. Or of the artists like Holberg, with lyrical melodies that remind us of Norway's incredibly beautiful landscape, of the sound of the traditional Hardanger fiddle. Grieg's most famous work was the music he wrote for Henrik Ibsen's play, Peer Gynt, the story of the Norwegian anti-hero who lived in Rondane and by the motto "to thine own self be true". He travelled around the world, but in the end he managed to return to his lost paradise in the forests and mountains of Rondane. Some of the melodies from *Peer Gynt,* such as "Morning Mood" and "Solveig's Song", have become immortal. Grieg lived at Troldhaugen for 22 years with his wife, Nina, until his death in 1907, at the age of 64. He is buried in the garden next to Nina, as he desired, where the evening sun's last rays shine. In the modern museum, opened in 1995, we can learn about the most important moments in Grieg's life through photographs and documents. The Victorian mansion is preserved as it was when the composer lived there. You will see many of his personal belongings, the dining room dominated by a magnificent Steinway grand piano and a beautiful portrait of Grieg and Nina. A small walkway leads us to the lake where Grieg had a small, red-painted hut built where he sat alone to compose in harmony with the environment. There is also a modern auditorium with 200 seats, a fine example of Scandinavian architecture, which holds concerts and other events, especially during the Bergen International Festival.

Troldhaugen, Edvard Grieg's estate.

Stalheim hotel.

6. WESTERN NORWAY: FROM BERGEN TO KRISTIANSUND

We follow E16, an example of the modernization of the network of roads in Norway, which quickly takes us north.

At **Gudvangen** we run into in the county of **Sogn og Fjordane**, which has an area of 18.620 km² and 108,000 inhabitants. Among the county's towns, we can mention Florø and Førde, each with approx. 12,000 inhabitants. Of all the outdoor experiences the county has to offer, Sognefjord is likely the most impressive, "The king of the fjords" extends 204 km inland and is the longest and deepest fjord in the world. Its greatest depth is 1398 metres. Furthermore, we can admire Nordfjord with Europe's largest mainland glacier, Jostedalsbreen, and the two national parks Jostedalsbreen and Jotunheimen. A totally unique natural environment, which can also be enjoyed from the Flåm Railway, one of the wildest and most beautiful train journeys in the world.

On the way to Sognefjorden we see the magnificent **Tvindefossen**. A little later we come to **Stalheim Hotel**, where there is a magnificent view over Nærøydalen. Down in the valley during the summer we can drive up one of the most thrilling roads, **Stalheimskleiva**, an old road that really requires the driver's attention. It was built over 150 years ago and has a number of very tight turns and powerful waterfalls on both sides. With a maximum climb of almost 20%, it is Norway's steepest and the sheerest stretch in Europe north of the Alps.

At Gudvangen we meet a narrow branch of Sognefjorden, Sognefjorden is on UNESCO list of World Heritage Sites. Because of the area's incredible natural beauty it is one of the premier tourist destinations in Norway for foreigners. In Gudvangen in the summer you can take a ferry to **Flåm**, the head of the Aurlandfjorden, or

Fjærland.

Urnes Stave Chuch.

Kaupanger on the north side of the fjord. By car or bus; the trip continues through the tunnels of the E16 to **Flåm, Aurland, Lærdal** and **Borgund**, including through the spectacular Lærdal Tunnel, the longest in the world at 24.5 kilometres. In summer we also recommended the old road over the mountains from Aurland to Lærdal, the "Snow Road". There is a National Tourist road where snow lies far into the summer, and which also has a great viewof Aurlandfjorden.

Borgund stave church is the most perfect and best preserved of all the Norwegian stave churches. Another interesting place is Urnes by Lustrafjord. Here is **Urnes Stave Church**, built around 1100 and the world's oldest church. The scenery around this area is so great that it is difficult to choose which route you should take, as they all are equally beautiful, interesting and exciting. A route which for many years has been very popular among tourists from every country, is called "Norway in a Nutshell". This is a day that lasts all day and that starts and ends in Bergen. It combines the train, boat and bus, and we pass through the most beautiful and magnificent fjord landscapes. If you do not have so much time available, this is the best choice. The excursion begins with a train

Flåm Railway

journey from Bergen to Myrdal. It switches over to the **Flåm Railway**, which runs from Myrdal to Flam. The train runs down along the waterfalls, rivers and lush vegetation. After 45 minutes and 20 km with a difference of

height of 867 metres behind us with an average slope of 5%. In Flåm the train stops at the pier and the passengers embark on a fantastic cruise on Aurlandfjorden and Nærøyfjorden. You go ashore in Gudvangen to

Flåm.

continue by bus to Stalheim Hotel up the winding Stalheimskleiva. Back at Voss, passengers travel back to Bergen by train.

From Gudvangen in the summer we can take the ferry to Kaupanger, on the northwest side of the fjord. You cross **Nærøyfjorden** which is the narrowest of these fjord branches. It also offers a unique combination of nature, flora and fauna, snow, ice and water, small farms and the old post road from Bergen to Oslo. The tour provides everlasting memories of absolute seductive beauty.. If we are lucky, on clear sunny days, we can pass seals sunbathing on the large boulders. **Balestrand**, which has an almost paradise-like beautiful natural environment, is one of Norway's most popular tourist destination, and a meeting place for artists, "celebrities" and tourists. Typical of this environment is **Kviknes Hotel**, built in 1877 in traditional Norwegian style, one of the few remaining examples of this style.

Borgund Stave Church.

Balestrand: Sognefjord Aquarium and Kviknes Hotel.

Olden.

Oldevatnet.

County Road 13 (National Tourist Road) from Balestrand over Gaularfjellet to Førde and Motorway 5 to Skei takes us north to Jostedalsbreen and Nordfjord.

Jostedalsbreen National Park has an area of 1.310 km². The glacier is 487 km² and is Europe's largest mainland. It is a great, compact, bluish mass of ice. In Norway, there are over 1600 glaciers. It is believed that the glacier has 24 large branches; one of the most popular is the one in Briksdalen. The excursion to Briksdalen is the most interesting in Nordfjord. To get to the foot of the glacier you must take motorway 60 to **Olden**, then turn towards Briksdalen. Driving further on Motorway 60, we come to the beautiful place **Loen**. On clear days you can see an almost perfect reflection of the snow-capped peaks and waterfalls in the sea.

One can go by foot to the **Briksdalsbreen**. It takes approx. 45 minutes, or we can drive the "Troll-car". The road up to the incredible blue-black ice sheet goes past waterfalls. You become totally overwhelmed by these forces of nature, and at the same time you can notice the continuing melting of the glaciers that have been occurring in recent years because of climate change.

The crashing of the ice and pieces that fall off remind us that glaciers are constantly moving. It is dangerous to walk on them without being accompanied by an expert and the right equipment.

We continue to **Stryn**, the largest settlement in Nordfjord, hub and tourist centre, and well known as an outstanding summer skiing centre. In Stryn, the road along the lakes towards **Oppstryn**, past **Jostedalsbreen**

On the "Troll-car" up to Briksdal Glacier.

Oppstryn.

National Park Centre with exhibits and films about the glacier and its flora and fauna. Here you can also get all the other information and support you require. We begin the ascent to **Strynefjellet** - 1000 metres above sea level. From the lush landscape on the fjord and lakes at Stryn, we come to a typical mountain landscape, barren and covered in snow and ice most of the year.

We have just entered **Møre og Romsdal** County, an area of 15.104 km², with 257,000 inhabitants. The cities are Ålesund, Molde and Kristiansund, all of which are surrounded by magnificent scenery. The county's longest fjord is Storfjorden, 110 km long, but the most famous is arguably Geirangerfjorden. Other things to experience are Trollstigen and the Atlantic Road. Here begins the so-called "Golden route", the route on which the royal couple chose to celebrate their 25th silver wedding along with the heads of the other European royal houses.

The road from Geiranger goes through a wild landscape and ends in **Dalsnibba**, 1,500 metres above sea level. It is one of the highest points you can reach by car in northern Europe, with a stunning view of the Sunnmørsalps. In the distance we can see the end of Geirangerfjorden. We drive down a winding road towards the fjord and come to **Flydalsjuvet**. From here we can admire one of the most famous prospects, not just in Geiranger, but in all of Norway. The fjord is surrounded by high mountains, ferries and cruise ships that are anchored at the bottom of the fjord.

Geirangerfjorden is 15 km long and is a UNESCO World Heritage Site. On the opposite side is **Ørneveien** that climbs 620 metres in 8 km. This road is a challenge for most drivers, and the only one that is open all year. On the ride around the fjord, you will feel the force and pressure from the vertical walls that threaten to slide into the fjord. This makes them seem

Geirangerfjorden.

even higher, while at the same time we hear the roar of the waterfalls. Here you can admire the famous waterfall "The Seven Sisters" (seven great "ponytails" plunging into the fjord). On the opposite side the wild "suitor" runs downwards. You can also see the abandoned farms, even a well-known pulpit, and lush vegetation where eagles and other birds have nests. Sometimes – like in Nærøyfjord – you might also be lucky enough to see the muzzle of a lonely seal or playful dolphins who have ventured

Geirangerfjorden seen from Flydalsjuvet.

Hellesylt.

into the fjord. Geirangerfjorden is all extremely intense and especially, almost excessively, beautiful.

We arrive at **Hellesylt** and continue along the fjord on the County Road 60 among magnificent mountains, until we get to **Storfjord**. On the way, we drive past **Stranda**, a small and quiet village on the shores of the bay that according to statistics has Norway's highest per capita income. A pretty impressive bit of information if one takes into account that Norway is one of the countries in the world with the highest standard of living.

From **Aursnes** we cross Storfjorden to **Magerholm**, towards Ålesund. Before we get there, we see a sign showing the way to another place not to be missed, namely **Trollstigen**.

Åndalsnes.

Trollstigen.

This fabulous hairpin road, located approx. 100 km from Ålesund on County Road 63, has recently been improved. The road is only open from May to September, and is one of the most incredible stretches of road you can drive on in Norway. We can go back and forth from Ålesund, or run on the way to Dombås on E136 through Romsdalen. An experience that is well worth trying. Trollstigen has always been the road that has connected Sunnmøre to Romsdalen. The road has eleven hairpin turns going up a slope that varies between 10% and 12% up to a height of 852 metres. Midway, right on the bridge at **Stigfossen**, is a magnificent view. At the top there are several breathtaking viewpoints over narrow valleys and the coast at **Åndalsnes**. There is also a new visitor centre with a restaurant and a small museum that shows how the road was built. At the restaurant, we eat some tasty, hot porridge. It may come in handy if it is windy and stormy, which are quite common in this area.

The bravest and most athletic can go all the way up, or down, on a trail that winds along the road. If you want still more nature, when you see Trollveggen you will lack neither the courage or desire, you can go 20 km inland where you'll find **Trolltind** and **Trollveggen.** The latter shoots straight upwards, 1,795 feet high, and looks incredibly impressive when you stand at the bottom. This is also a mountain climber's paradise. **Trollveggen** is and has always been immensely popular among hang gliders and base jumpers, but after several fatal accidents it is now forbidden to jump from here.

Do not go straight to the city centre when you get to **Ålesund** (44 000 inhabitants), but follow the signs to Aksla mountain, a vantage point that is 150 metres above the city. From here you get a view few cities can offer. From the city, there is a staircase with 418 steps up to this vantage point. On top you can admire the distinctive planning. Ålesund town centre is built on three islands connected by bridges. The city lies between the ocean and the fjord, surrounded by small towns, mountains and islands - a sight you will never forget. The

Ålesund from Aksla.

city's architecture is also distinctive, as the city burned down one stormy winter night in 1904. 10,000 were left homeless, but the town was rebuilt in three years, in Jugendstil.

Ålesund is the largest city in Møre og Romsdal County and one of the most important fishing ports. Hurtigruten ("The Express Ship Route") is also here. The city has a lot of industrial activity related to the fishing industry. When we walk along the streets, we can sense something Venetian from the canals. We can study the short-lived but interesting Jugend architecture closer. A style which presents itself here with towers and spires, beautiful floral motifs and extravagant and unusual facades. The Jugendstil centre is a national centre for Art Nouveau/Jugendstil.

The centre is located in the preserved Apotekergården. A visit here is highly recommended. Among those who later helped with the reconstruction was Emperor Wilhelm II of Germany. He sent a lot of building materials, among other things. After WWII, many people wanted to change the name of one of the city's main streets - Kaiser Wilhelms gate. Anything that smacked of German was not popular then.

Ålesund had its own opinion on the matter, and the street retained its original name. Take a walk and enjoy the marine, half bohemian atmosphere of Ålesunds streets while admiring the architecture's big and little details.

If you want to know more about the

Ålesund centre.

Art Nouveau style houses in Ålesund.

city, its history and development, visit the Ålesund Museum, the Sunnmøre museum or the Fisheries Museum. You should not forget to take a trip to Atlanterhavsparken, a modern aquarium with large exhibition tanks depicting fish species and their habitat. If you want to see more of the coast, boats leave from the harbour which take you out to the islands and fishing villages. One of the most interesting islands is **Runde,** which with more than 40 different bird species and a million nesting birds is a paradise for ornithologists.

The road north along the coast goes past mountains and lakes, over sea and land, over bridges and on ferries. Finally we come to **Molde** (25,000 inhabitants), the City of Roses. Roses so far north? Hard to believe, but true.

The island of Grip outside Kristiansund.

6. Western Norway: from Bergen to Kristiansund

Molde was founded in 1742, but there is little left of the old town, which was bombed by the Germans in 1940. Molde is today a new, open city with large parks where roses are proud to thrive so far north. There is always life on the streets, and even more in

Molde.

June during the jazz festival. Molde's surroundings are especially beautiful. Follow the signs to **Varden**, a vantage point 407 metres above sea level. With the city below, on clear days you can see the Romsdal Mountains. They consist of 87 snowy peaks which lay like a pearl necklace along the fjord, the city as a brooch.

If we continue along the coastal road, we come to a feat of Norwegian engineering: **Atlanterhavsveien** ("Atlantic Road"). It was opened in 1992 and is open all year round. The road has eight bridge spans and connects the eight islands with the mainland. The project was initiated due to several accidents in the area over the years. At the entrance between the first and second islands, there is an information area where you can look beyond the road and see the barren and windswept coastline. It is a very special and unique experience as the stormy days can be quite exciting when high waves spill over the road and bridge.

The Atlantic Road.

Kristiansund.

On the way to Kristiansund, it is a good idea to stop at the **Kvernes stavkirke** on Averøy. This is a well kept and beautiful church which is in a rural setting.

We arrive at **Kristiansund** (24,000 inhabitants) via Atlanterhavstunnelen, 700 metres long and 250 metres deep, to the three islands that make up the city. Kristiansund was founded by King Christian IV at the same time as Molde. Right from the beginning the fish has been the basis of its economy. Cod from Lofoten was cut up and dried in large flakes dried fish, the basis for the famous and tasty "bacalao". There is always a lot of activity in and around the harbour and pedestrian streets. The statues of "Klippfiskkjerringa" (the Clipfish woman) and "Sildegutten" (the Herring boy) are a tribute to Kristiansund's past and symbolize the city's commerce.

There is not much left of the old Kristiansund, since the city was bombed during the war. Today the city streets are modern and impersonal commercial streets like in many other Norwegian cities. The city certainly has interesting things to offer, such as Nordmøre Museum, the beautiful islands that face the ocean, and an active cultural life (the famous, annual Opera Week). You must not forget Vardetårnet, a tower with views of the mountains in Nordmøre, the Romsdal mountains in the distance, the city and the harbour.

On our way north after driving over an impressive bridge over **Tingvollfjorden**, and after taking the ferry at Kanestraumen to Halsa, we finally come to Trøndelag and are headed for Trondheim.

The Eidsvoll Building in Eidsvoll.

7. CENTRAL NORWAY: FROM OSLO TO TRONDHEIM

On its long way to the north, E6 runs parallel to the Swedish border and throughout the eastern part of the country. The landscape is rural and quiet, and alternates between spruce and pine forests and cornfields, farms and towns. This is Hedmark. From Oslo, we drive through Akershus past **Eidsvoll**. Here we can visit the Eidsvoll Building, where the Norwegian constitution was written and signed on May 17th, 1814. We then drive along **Mjøsa**, Norway's largest and third-deepest lake. The whole landscape comes together and is reflected in the lake. The road continues along the shore, and we come to **Hamar**. Here we find one of the Winter Olympics' architectural gems, the skating stadium **Vikingskipet**, with a great Scandinavian design, shaped like the inverted keel of a Viking ship. The building is currently used as sports stadium among other things. The old episcopal city (Hamar is one of Norway's oldest towns) also has impressive cathedral ruins, a folk museum, an emigrant museum and the country's only railway museum. Our world famous opera singer **Kirsten Flagstad** was born and raised here and her home is opened to visitors.

After crossing Mjøsa, we come to the exit to **Gjøvik**, a nice little town in Oppland, where an impressive sports stadium in the mountains, mainly for hockey, was built for the Olympic Winter Games in 1994.

Approximately eight kilometres outside Lillehammer you can find the best view of the lake, the city and the Olympic Centre. Sometimes we can also see the famous paddle steamer **Skibladner** out on the

Hamar.

The Viking Ship stadium in Hamar.

Paddle steamer Skibladner at the quay in Hamar.

water. Skibladner, built in 1856, is the world's oldest paddle-steamer still in operation, and is called "Mjøsa's white swan". Lillehammer, which is where Mjøsa and Gudbrandsdalen meet, is a beautiful city of 26,800 inhabitants. The town has been a popular tourist destination both in summer and winter since the 1850's, thanks to its great location.

The city is located up a hill, proud of its old wooden houses and typical streets. Especially Storgata, which is a pedestrian street that is always

Lillehammer.

Lillehammer.

full of people, surrounded by older, renovated buildings. A paradise for those who are looking for typical Norwegian products and souvenirs.

In Lillehammer we find the second of the country's largest folk museums, **Maihaugen**. It has a collection of 200 buildings from Gudbrandsdalen. They were saved from destruction and oblivion by Dr. Sandvig, a renowned dentist who lived and worked most of his life in the city. At the museum you can see how the Norwegians lived and worked in the past. The most famous structure is stave church from Garmo, built around the year 1200 and moved to the museum in 1921. When it was still in Garmo, our world-renowned Nobel Prize winner, author Knut Hamsun, was baptized there.

But what draws many tourists to the city it the **Olympic Park**, where many of the major events of the Olympic Games were held in 1994. Here we can enter the Olympic Stadium where the opening and closing ceremonies were held, admire two big jumps with

Storgata in Lillehammer.

Maihaugen.

Lysgårdsbakken, opening of the Olympic Games in 1994.

Lillehammer Olympiapark.

lengths of 90 and 120 metres, and walk or take the cable car up to the tower, where there is a magnificent view over the whole area. We can also see Håkon Hall, which today is used for various types of sporting events, and also contains a Olympic Museum. Hockey matches were played in it before the previously mentioned mountain stadium in Gjøvik.

Back on the E6 we follow the river Gudbrandsdalslågen north and come to **Hunderfossen Familiepark**,

an amusement park for the whole family with more than 50 different entertainment offerings. Here you can meet inhabitants of the Norwegian forests – the trolls! In the middle of the park is the Norway's tallest troll. It is made of fibreglass, is 14 metres high and weighs 70 tons. It was created by Ivo Caprino. Throughout the country, stories and fairy tales are told about trolls; sometimes they do foolish antics, sometimes they are bad. Trolls are pretty ugly, with big noses and very old. Some are big, others are almost dwarfs, but all are extremely strong and never have good intentions. They live in the forests and mountains of the country. They come alive at night but during the day they turned back into trees or boulders. It's no wonder that in a country like Norway, with all its the rocks, dense forests, fog and snow, you see silhouettes that become trolls in the imagination.

The Family Park was constructed at this location because it is precisely in the dense forests and mountains of Oppland and Hedmark where many fairy tales about trolls originated. From here, the stories spread across the country. This is why you will find more than one giant troll figure who greets you with a teasing smile. They are found in Dombås, in Grong and many other places.

We follow the river north with the road always running parallel with the railway line to Trondheim. We see towns, farms and churches which all have their own story. This

Hunderfossen theme park: water park and the giant troll.

Sognefjellet, Jotunheimen National Park.

Styggebreen, Glacier at Galdhøpiggen.

was the route the pilgrims took to Trondheim to honour St. Olav's tomb. Meanwhile the landscape becomes wilder and steeper, and it gets longer between houses. We are still in **Gudbrandsdalen** - the most magnificent of all Norway's inland valleys and the most full of tradition. In the northernmost part, the valley is surrounded by **Jotunheimen** on one side and **Rondane** on the other. These mountains are both national parks.

In **Ringebu** we find one of the country's major stave churches, with a stunning decor and a Baroque altar, surrounded by a peaceful churchyard. From here there is a magnificent view out over the valley. The church at Ringebu is still in use as the parish church, and the church in this parish that has the most weddings.

In Vinstra we find the Peer Gynt road, which runs through the mountains where the Norwegian hero lived. In

Rondane National Park.

summer the Peer Gynt Festival is held in beautiful surroundings on the banks of Gålåvatn. For a whole week you can attend exciting productions of Ibsen's works, accompanied by the music of Edvard Grieg in the Nordic twilight.

We continue past **Otta** and **Dombås**, which is an important commercial centre and hub. From here we

"Furusjøen" lake at Rondane National Park.

Snøhetta in Dovrefjell National Park.

continue on E136 to Åndalsnes and Trollstigen, Ålesund and the fjords of western Norway, or on the E6 to Trondheim, which is 200 km further north.

We continue north. The road goes over **Dovrefjell** and climbs higher. Spruce, pine and birch disappear, and at the top the landscape is pretty barren. This is the outer edge

Røros.

of the **Dovrefjell National Park**, the only place in Norway where you can see Musk oxen, a species of bison or wisent - which was wiped out in Norway, but was reintroduced here with individual animals from Greenland.

On the way to Trondheim, we highly recommend paying a visit to Røros. An old mining town that is also included in the UNESCO list of humanity's cultural heritage.

Røros is located 600 metres above sea level. The municipality is 170 km^2 and has 5,600 inhabitants. The mining town was founded in 1644 by the Danish King Christian IV to extract and smelt copper from the mines. The king ordered a rectangular urban design for the town, and that all the buildings be built of wood. In the early 1900's, people became aware of the site's distinctive architectural and urban style. This initiated an extensive restoration of the city, which has now made Røros a model and one of Norway's most beautiful citiess.

From Røros we continue to

Røros church.

Trondheim, Norway's second oldest and third largest city, which has 177,000 inhabitants and is the administrative centre of Trøndelag. It is a university and industrial city,

Model of mines at Røros.

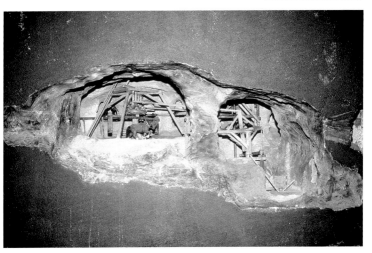

Trondheim.

Folk dance at Kristiansten Fortress. Trondheim in the background.

and is the country's historic capital. It is, thanks to one of Norway's most representative buildings, Nidarosdomen, and its religious, political and national significance.

The cathedral lies at the head of the Trondheimfjorden, at the mouth of **Nidelven**. The city was founded in 997 by King Olav Tryggvason, who set the royal residence here and made it the kingdom of Norway's most important city, where he also had the first cathedral built. This is why the statue of Olav, which shows a Viking king with a falcon and sword, stands in the marketplace and has become the city's symbol. It was Olav Haraldsson who finally managed to unit Norway into one kingdom by introducing Christianity to the country and creating a public administrative system. After his death at the battle of Stiklestad in 1030, his body was buried under the altar. Thus began the legend of St. Olav, who for 500 years attracted thousands of pilgrims from all over northern Europe. This meant that the city grew around the church, later Nidaros Cathedral, where many of the Norwegian kings have been crowned. The cathedral is also a mausoleum. More than fifteen kings, queens and princesses are buried here.

Nidaros Cathedral has gone through several phases. King Magnus the Good expanded the original church building. In 1093 Olav Kyrre ordered the construction of a Romanesque stone church. But it was in 1161 that Bishop Øystein Erlandsson laid the foundation for the present cathedral in Gothic style, inspired by the Anglo-Nordic Gothic architecture. In the following centuries, the cathedral suffered several fires, but was restored each time. After 1536, when Protestantism was introduced in Norway, the cathedral was plundered. The coffin containing the remains of St. Olav disappeared. That year marks the beginning of the decay of the Nidaros Cathedral.

The city was destroyed by a fire in 1681, and was rebuilt as it appears today according to a town design developed by Gaspar de Cicignon. The real city's real growth began in the 1800's. At that time it had 9,500 inhabitants, more than in Christiania, and the city had a very busy harbour. There was also a vibrant intellectual community, thanks to the Royal Norwegian Scientific Company and the nation's first theatre and newspaper. After 1905, when the union with Sweden was dissolved, the city regained its importance as an historic capital with the coronation of King Håkon VII. The last king who was crowned here was King Harald V, 23 June 1991.

The main street is **Munkegata**, which connects the harbour, where there is a fish market everyday, with **Torvet**, the market square, where there is a statue of **Olav Tryggvason**. On the left side, before arriving at the square, is **Stiftsgården**, Scandinavia's largest wooden building and today the King's residence when he is in town. Close to the square is the beautiful Romanesque **Vår Frue Kirke**.

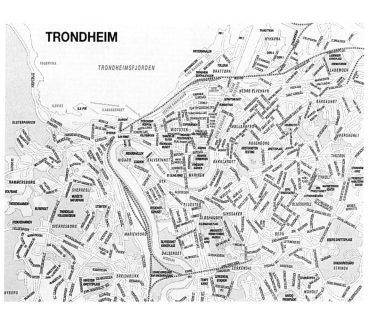

Statue of Olav Tryggvason and Vår Frue Church.

At the top of the street is **Nidarosdomen**, with its distinctive tower. You should definitely pay a visit to this cathedral, which has played a particularly important role in the history of Norway, and is one of Scandinavia's artistic gems.

The first overwhelming experience we get is from the facade that is illuminated by the afternoon sun. The facade consists of three rows of sculptures depicting historical figures from the Bible and the history of Norway, with kings and other legendary and allegorical figures. They are replicas of the originals that are in the Cathedral's museum.

You will no doubt find be fascinated by the Cathedral's interior dimensions: 102 x 50 x 21 metres. It has three ships and has preserved its original Gothic style. Go up towards the

Stiftsgården.

Nidaros Cathedrale

transept and notice how the Romanesque and Gothic church comes together in an admirable way. Continue towards the choir and see the brilliant architectural design Archbishop Erlandsson used to cover it: the octagon. Continue your wandering about to the main altar, you see the holy spring on the left, where hundreds of thousands of pilgrims for 500 years drank and crossed themselves, as well as the capitals.

Gamle bybro (Old City Bridge).

Stroll around the main ship and see once again the how impressive the structure is, the beautiful stained glass windows, the large rose window, and the organ. The Cathedral also has first-class acoustics. At night in the summer months, evenings of song, declamations and concerts are held here. The programme is especially interesting during the St. Olav Festival. If you are available, we recommend that you attend one of these to experience the unique atmosphere of the Cathedral.

Next to the church is **Bispegården**, built in the 1200s. It is Scandinavia's largest secular building in the Gothic style, and a testament to the power and authority of the Archbishop of Nidaros had, as head of the Norwegian church in Norway, the Faroe Islands, Shetland, the Orkney Islands, Iceland and Greenland.

When we leave the Cathedral, we can proceed to the **Old Town Bridge**, which crosses the river Nidelva. Here is the river harbour with old warehouses built on pontoons,

restored and converted into homes and offices and painted in vibrant reds reflected in the river Nidelva. On sunny days, it is one of the most beautiful sights in the city.

On summer evenings, there is a lot going on in this area and in the harbour. This is where the pubs, cafes and bars are where you can enjoy a beer and shrimp while the light Nordic summer night buzzes with talk and laughter, interrupted only by seagulls or somebody singing.

Trondheim has plenty of interesting culture to offer. The city has ten museums and many art galleries. We especially recommend the **NTNU Vitenskapsmuseet**, (the Museum of Natural History and Archaeology) one of the institutions most heavily involved in collecting the city's history. The museum is divided into several different sections that depict the city's history, religious art, natural history, archeology ethnography and numismatics (coin science). The music history section is particularly interesting.

Trøndelag Folk Museum

Outside the city is the **Ringve Museum** and the **Trøndelag Folk Museum**. The first is located in a mansion from the early 1800's and contains a large collection of ancient musical instruments. The second is an open air museum with 60 buildings from past centuries that have been

Ringve museum.

Munkholmen outside of Trondheim.

relocated here from all over the region. Do not miss the stave church and the inn **The Tavern,** a house from 1739, where typical Norwegian food is still served.

Before leaving Trondheim, we can admire the city one last time from two different viewpoints. **Tyholttårnet** is 120 metres high and has a revolving restaurant 74 metres above the ground, and from **Sverresborg** you have an magnificient view of the city, the fjord and the mountains surrounding the country and the historical, religious and symbolic centre, Nidarosdomen. We can also take a trip out to the little island **Munkholmen** located in Trondheimfjorden. On Munkholmen executions were carried out until the 1100s, when a Benedictine abbey was built there. After the Reformation, this was turned into a fortress that today is an interesting place to visit. The E6 leaving Trondheim goes in turns through the beautiful countryside along Trondheimfjorden and always parallel to the railway line. We continue north through the coastal landscape which is also rural, with several small towns, villages, farms, an occasional church, chapel and war monuments, harbours, agricultural land, pine and birch forests. All in a natural, beautiful and surprising fusion. The harmony of the landscape gives off a sense of calm. The idyllic scenes follow each other, but we should not forget how hard the Norwegian climate can treat this area. About 100 kilometres north is **Stiklestad** in Verdalen. Here was the battle that cost St. Olav his life July 29th, 1030. Stiklestad is today a national cultural centre. Around the chapel that covers the stone where St. Olav was killed is a Folk Museum and an open air theatre where "The St. Olav Play" is performed at the St. Olav Festival (last week of July and first of August). The performance uses 200 actors for music, dance, song and battle scenes, in the tradition of the great religious medieval plays and draws thousands of spectators each year.

The best representative of the idyllic scenery in central Norway is the landscape around **Snåsavatn**. It is the largest lake in this region, which is a rural, desolate and uninhabited world. We recommend driving the E6 and continuing along the south end of the lake. There you will see nearly virgin landscape with the occasional farmhouse. In the spring, half of the ground is coloured by the intense yellow of the rapeseed flower, which competes with the green forests and the bright blue of the lakes and the colours on the palette of a passionate painter. Here we can admire **Bolareinen**, Central Norway's largest collection of petroglyphs. There are many remnants of these rock carvings in the whole region, as well as in northern Norway. The carvings show how prehistoric people lived and hunted, and what they believed in. It is believed that these drawings, dating back to 3,000 years BC or earlier, had a magical significance for hunting and trapping.

After **Grong** we continue along **Namsen**, one of the country's most salmon-rich rivers, where it fishing competitions are often held. We drive past **Fiskumfossen**, an impressive waterfall of 35 metres, where

Stiklestad during St. Olav Festival.

previously you could see the salmon jump during the spawning season. After a power plant and a dam were built across the river, this was no longer possible. The authorities have therefore installed tubing under the earth, the longest of its kind in the world, so that salmon could get past the waterfall. In this place we find **Namsen Salmon Aquarium**. It is small but has excellent platforms and terraces where you can observe the new facility and the always fascinating jumping salmon during the spawning season. The place is highly recommended. It also serves a tasty buffet of all types of salmon of outstanding quality.

Fishing in Namsen.

Mosjøen.

8. NORTHEN-NORWAY: FROM MOSJØEN TO BODØ

Northern-Norway

This large and pristine area of approx. 113.000 km² covers a third of mainland Norway's territory and consists of the counties of Nordland, Troms and Finnmark. Northern Norway has around 470,000 inhabitants, i.e., 10% of the population. The harsh climate and long winters is probably the explanation for the fact that the further north you go, the fewer people there are. In Nordland, the population density is 6.7 per km², in Troms 5.2 and Finnmark, 1.6.

After the Second World War, the northern part of the country was almost totally destroyed. When the Germans retreated, they practiced a scorched earth policy, which meant that almost all of Finnmark and half of Troms were destroyed. Those residents who did not manage to hide were forced to flee south. After peace in 1945, most moved back up north again, and the reconstruction of the region occurred at a rapid pace. After 1960, a new industrial development began with the construction of several factories in Mosjøen, Mo i Rana and Troms. Later a rapid development began along the coast due to the discovery of oil. The fishing industry had a boom, with a third of all catches in the country, and the region has an important canning and frozen fish industry.

Despite the industrial and urban

growth, northern Norway is known for preserving its natural surroundings in a unique way. Thanks to the Gulf Stream there is a relatively mild climate along the coast, while the interior is cold and harsh. The average temperature in winter in Lofoten is -2 degrees Celsius, but on the plateau, temperatures can go down to -40 degrees Celsius; the country's lowest temperature of nearly -55 was measured here. Vegetation and flora are therefore also different. When the midnight sun shines in summer, it colours the mountains and the sea in all shades of yellow, from pale orange to almost red. During the winter, the polar night is interrupted by the Northern Lights in a magical way, which gives the snow and ice a scarlet red silver colour.

From Mosjøen to Bodø

Nordland is a long stretched out county of over 38,000 km² with 240,000 inhabitants Bodø is the largest city in Nordland, with 48,500 inhabitants, followed by Mo i Rana and Narvik. Narvik is known from WWII. Other towns are Mosjøen, Fauske, Sortland and Svolvaer. Nordland is the northernmost county thait has tbe most industries, and therefore most residents.

From the south, we come first to Helgeland, who has a rugged coastline and slightly undulating inland with lush vegetation. **Mosjøen** is the first settlement here. Here, Sjøgata is worth a visit. Approximately 50 km south of Mosjøen you can drive out to the Brønnøysund and Vega Islands.

Mo i Rana, northern Norway's third largest city, was reconstructed after the war around state-owned ironworks. But it is now a lively commercial city "The City below the Arctic Circle." You have to take a trip around Moholmen and Havmannen. We proceed to the area around the

Mo i Rana.

Glacier hiking on Svartisen.

Arctic Circle, Saltfjellet. The landscape surprises us again: **Svartisen** with its 370 km ², is Norway's second largest glacier. Svartisen and Saltfjellet are national parks. Here you can visit one of Scandinavia's most interesting limestone caves, **Grønligrotta**, or take a boat over Svartisvatn and hike up a two-mile trail to the foot of the Svartisen, an incredible sight.

We come then to the **Arctic Circle**. An imaginary line that runs along 66

Svartisen.

degrees and 33 minutes north, which is the gateway to the earth's cold northern latitudes, to the land of the midnight sun. There is a different, special and dramatic coexistence between man and nature here.

The midnight sun is a phenomenon that can be observed between 50 and 70 days a year, which is visible throughout the northern part of Scandinavia, depending on what latitude you find yourself at. This phenomenon is due to several concurrent factors. The shift of the Earth's rotation axis, compression of the poles and the Earth's motion around the sun meaning that the sun does not go down below the horizon during the summer in these latitudes. You go over to the next day without losing sight of the sun. It looks as if the sun is hanging over the horizon, and after midnight it begins to rise again.

In the winter we get the reverse effect. For 50-70 days the sun never comes over the horizon, and we get the long polar night, when you can only see a very faint light on the horizon. That's when we can see the phenomenon known as the Northern Lights; sun particles attracted to poles by magnetic force collide with the upper layers of the atmosphere and produce a friction which creates the Northern Lights.

To mark our crossing the Arctic Circle, a **Polar Circle Centre** has been built in a desolate landscape of mountains, snow and boulders. A large igloo with a cafeteria, a shop, and museum that displays a wonderful collage of Northern Norway. Moreover, there is also a post office that stamps postcards with a special stamp which is proof that you have been there!

If you want to feel special in this unique and desolate place, where the wind, the cold, ice and snow rule, you should take a walk around the area and experience the magnificent scenery. You can also follow an old Nordic tradition and honour Mother Earth by building a stone altar in her honour. You will see that yours is not the only one. You can also find

Arctic Circle Centre.

Saltstraumen.

monuments that remind us of the prisoners who died here while they built railways and roads during the war.

E6 goes down to the beautiful and green **Saltfjorden**. We drive past **Fauske**, a major hub where there are the most marble quarries in Norway. This marble was used in the Oslo City Hall and the United Nations building in New York.

In Fauske, the E6 goes further north towards Tysfjord Ofoten and Narvik. If we follow motorway 80 we come to Bodø and the islands. Nordlandsbanen, which the Germans made prisoners build from Trondheim, 700 km further south, also goes to Bodø, where it ends. From here there is only a vehicle road for the many miles remaining to North Cape.

We continue along Saltfjord to Bodø.

On the other side of the fjord you can see Børvasstindene and the bridge over Saltstraumen.

We recommend you pay a visit to one of the great natural wonders of the area which is about 30 km south of Bodø, **Saltstraumen**, also known as the abyss, is the world's strongest ocean current, and inspired writers such as Edgar Allan Poe and Jules Verne. The flow begins in Lofoten, between the islands of Moskenes and Værøy, and reaches its peak in a narrow passage between two fjords, which is three miles long and 150 feet wide. When the current is the strongest it can lead 372 million m³ of water at a speed of 14 metres per second. It creates some incredible whirlpools with a diameter of five to ten metres, leading tons of small fish into the little fjord where fishermen and seagulls

Bodø.

Bodø harbour.

are waiting - a fishermen's paradise. This phenomenon is dependent on the tides and position of the moon. It occurs four times a day, six hours in each direction, two in and two out. Check the times and try to see it when the current is flowing inward. Saltstraumen is always different, and always makes an impression. You can observe the phenomenon from the shores of the bay, or from the great bridge that goes from bank to bank.

Bodø is the Nordland's largest city with 48,500 inhabitants, and is a major hub, the gateway both by air and by sea to Lofoten and Vesterålen. It is an active commercial city, with an important fishing related industry. A large part of the "nightlife" here takes place in shopping centres and the protected harbour. On sunny days, residents and tourists walk among the boats, kiosks and shrimp sellers. If the weather is bad, it's pretty empty in the streets. Such are the contrasts in northern Norway.

Bodø, the city of the eagles, has Europe's largest eagle colony. As a city and architecturally speaking, Bodø is relatively impersonal. The city was founded in 1816 and experienced increasing economic growth based on the herring fishery in the western area, as well as because of a trade rivalry with Bergen. On the night of May 27, 1940 the city was bombed by the Germans and almost completely destroyed. After reconstruction, it became a bustling centre of commerce and industry, which is heavily influenced by the nearby air base and civilian airport.

Among the sights we want to mention **Bodin Church**, which has a pear-shaped bell tower, the interesting and modern **Norwegian Aviation Museum**, with sections that display both military and civil aviation, and the **Nordland Museum**, which has Archaeology and history sections, as well as one about the Vikings. We will also mention the pier at **Kjerringøy**, where there are fifteen finely restored buildings depicting the area's past as a fishing and trading port.

From **Rønvikfjellet**, 150 metres high, there is a magnificent view of the city, coast, mountains and the islands in the background. In the light of the midnight sun, between May 30th and July 12th, it is a particularly fascinating landscape.

Bodø: Aviation Museum

Kjerringøy.

"Lofot fiske" in Lofoten.

9. NOTHERN NORWAY: LOFOTEN, VESTERÅLEN AND NARVIK

Besides the fjords of western Norway, Lofoten and Vesterålen have the largest outdoor experiences to offer in Norway. These are two island groups located approx. 200 km north of the Arctic Circle. They are formed by geological materials of different origin and age.

Lofoten consists of six islands. Two of them, Værøy and Røst, can only be reached by helicopter, airplane or boat. The other four, Moskenes, Flakstad, Vågøy and Austvågøy, have good road access via bridges and tunnels on E10, also known as King Olavs vei. The group of islands has an area of 1.227 km² and about 25,000 inhabitants. Svolvaer, located on the northernmost island, is the region's administrative centre.

The boat from Bodø to Moskenes takes 3 hours and 45 minutes, and 4 hours and 30 to minutes Stamsund and Svolvær. On the trip across Vestfjorded you can see **Lofotenveggen**, an impressive mountain range with jagged, bare peaks that are 100 km long. At the foot of the wall are the small fishing boats, fishermen, cabins, skerries, fields and beaches of white sand - in short, a unique blend of an ever changing coastal, inland and mountain scenery. This just in the few kilometres that separates the east coast from the west coast. A landscape where man and nature have lived in harmony for centuries.

The primitive man who lived on these islands fished and hunted. It was the Vikings who really left their mark with trading activities in Nordland. In the mid-1800s, after Bergen lost the trade monopoly that the city had in this area, fisheries began to really pick up. In the late 1800's, when the Hurtigruten (Express ship route) was created, the islands got daily connection to the mainland.

Fish is the island's most important commodity. The world's largest cod bank is in Lofoten. Thanks to the Gulf Stream, temperatures in Lofoten are high enough that the cod can multiply. In November and December, the seven to ten year old fish leave the Barents Sea to spawn in warmer water. This happens in Lofoten, where the so-called **Lofoten fishing** takes place from late January to mid-April.

The fishing goes on 24 hours a day without interruption. Afterwards, the fish is cleaned and cut. The head will be preserved and used for the soup, after the tongue is cut out. Deep fried cod tongues are a great delicacy. The rest of the fish is gutted and hung to dry. Afterwards it is salted, packed in boxes and exported. While fishing, the fishermen live in the so-called cabins. Most are painted red and are quite spartan. On our journey between the islands we find many small villages where we see the familiar silhouette of these cabins that with time have become a hallmark of Lofoten.

In recent years, tourism has become the second most important source of income for the islands. Lofoten is a paradise for all kinds of activity tourism, fishing, diving, sailing, hiking, biking, kayaking, etc. This is also a paradise for bird lovers. On **Værøy** and **Røst** there are the large colonies of gulls, cormorants and puffins. Most of the visitors who come to this region spend the night in the cabins.

If you do not have much time available, the best way to see the islands is to drive on E10 that winds between the steep mountains.

On Moskenes is **Reine**, without a doubt one of the most beautiful places in Norway, and the most photographed and painted. On

Lofoten.

Puffin at Røst.

113

Skomvær Lighthouse.

Reine in Lofoten.

Nusfjord.

the waterfront, there is a collection of cabins surrounded by majestic mountains. On the same island, at the foot of an imposing, triangular mountain lies the small, quaint harbour of **Hamnøy**.

On the island **Flakstad**, between white sand beaches and turquoise blue waters you can see a typical church with pear-shaped towers, and visit the island's most charming place, **Nusfjord**. It is located on a narrow cove and similar to both Old Stavanger and Røros was restored in 1975 in conjunction with the European Ecological year, as an example of the Norwegian fishermen's way of life. There is a collection of 30 red-and yellow-painted cabins from the 1800's in a circle around the harbour. Nusfjord smells of sea, cod, and everywhere there are seagulls that almost give us the feeling of being in a "Hitchcock" film. An unforgettable place!

We drive on to **Vestvågøy** through the tunnel under Nappstraumen. This island has the most agriculture. From **Leknes** we can continue to Stamsund, yet another charming fishing village, located on the east coast. If we continue on E10 through the only opening in the "Lofotveggen" between east and west, we drive past **Lofotr Viking Museum** at Borg, which has a great design and includes a replica of a Viking reception hall that was found in Nordland. It is 83 metres long and has a 9-foot ceiling. There are also interesting archaeological finds here and a replica of the Gokstad ship (the original is in Oslo). The road passes by fields, farms, lakes and animal herds. The landscape looks much more like the Swiss countryside than islands in the Norwegian Sea.

On Austvågøy we drive on a narrow road going between high mountains and rocks over two

Henningsvær.

suspension bridges until we come to **Henningsvær**, the Venice of Lofoten. Henningsvær is a small fishing village built on the three islands. The first car didn't arrive here until 1982. The landscape of the bridge, warehouses, and fishing boats with mountains in the background is also one of the most beautiful in Lofoten.

Henningsvær.

Svolvær with the mountain "Svolværgeita".

Kabelvåg is possibly the most visited place on the islands. It is located near the ancient Viking settlement Vågan. Here you will find the Lofoten Museum, a replica of a cabin from the 1700's, Lofot Aquarium and "Lofoten Cathedral", one of Northern Norway's largest wooden churches.

Svolvær is a hub for sea and air, and the islands' administrative, commercial and industrial centre. If you stop in the harbour, you can admire **Svolværgeita**, a cliff of 569 metres with two projections (horns) at the top, where experienced mountaineers end their climb with a jump from one horn to the other. A little larger is Leknes, also an important centre.

From Svolvær harbour, we can take

Trollfjorden.

a boat ride that lasts three hours to and from the **Trollfjorden**, Northern Norway's narrowest fjord, surrounded on both sides by vertical cliffs. Here the Hurtigruten ships sails on their way to Stokmarknes in Vesterålen. The "Battle of Trollfjord" occurred between the fishermen and the larger fishing companies in Bergen and Bodø in the early nineteenth century, with a tragic outcome. The battle is depicted in the famous painting that hangs in the town hall in Svolvaer, and in Johan Bojers book *The Last Viking.* While the E10 continues ferry-free to the mainland, we take a detour to the pier in Fiskebøl, where a ferry takes us to Melbu in Vesterålen. On the way we can admire Sildpollnes church that shines brightly both winter and summer. When we leave the islands, we can see flocks of gulls and puffins and solitary cormorants accompanying us on our journey. They are a living example of a noisy world that has remained unchanged.

Vesterålen archipelago consists of the islands Hadseløya, Langøya, Hinnøya, which is Norway's largest and Andøya, the most spectacular. The landscape is not as overwhelming as in Lofoten, but it contains many great surprises. The area is 2.368 km² and has 32,000 inhabitants. The administrative centre is **Sortland** but **Harstad** is the largest city.

From **Melbu** on Hadseløya, where one of Northern Norway's most important music festivals is held, we continue on Rv82 to **Stokmarknes**, which has an important harbour, where Captain Richard With founded the Hurtigruten company in 1893. There are also the **Hurtigruten Museum**.

We run into Langøya over two bridges and along Hadselfjord. On the other side, the majestic peaks of the Lofoten and Vesterålen rise up, along with Møysalen which is 1262 metres high. On Langøya there are small fishing villages, such as. **Nyksund**, which, in the 1900's, was

Stø in Vesterålen.

Vesterålens second largest fishing village, abandoned, revitalized - and now a popular destination for artists and tourists. Sortland is also here, which is the base for the Coast Guard in Northern Norway, and **Jennestad**, with its antique shops and warehouses. This is a calm and green landscape with quiet beaches with bird colonies on the cliffs. Farther north, there are whales and modern sculptures, like *The Man from the Sea,*

The northern lights above Andøya

Andenes lighthouse.

on the west coast. This figure is part of the collection **Artscape Nordland** and consists of 33 modern sculptures placed around the countryside in the county of Nordland. This is the earth, the landscape and the people that Knut Hamsun immortalized in his novels.

Andøya is for many reasons the most interesting island. Among other things, the landscape contrasts with the large flat areas to the east and steep mountains in the west. On **Bleiksøya** there is a very large bird colony with 400,000 gulls, puffins etc., which is the second largest

Whale safari.

in Norway. **Andenes** has a typical lighthouse and a great and famous harbour. From here, Captain Ahab set out on his hunt for Moby Dick in Melville's immortal novel. Here we also find several museums that have displays of the northern lights as well as the region's flora and fauna not to mention the **Whale Centre**. The centre offers tours of the whale world through slideshows with outstanding and interesting commentary from the centre guides and biologists. The visit also includes a whale safari in the Norwegian Sea, where you can experience the amazing spectacle of seeing whales diving with an elegant, unforgettable tail movement.

On Hinnøya is the islands most beautiful city, **Harstad**, with 23,000 residents. In Harstad there is lively trade in the port area, where Northern Norway's main shipyard is situated. The city is also considered the region's "cultural capital". In the modern cultural centre frequent festivals and artist performances are held. Of the city's attractions that we want to mention is Trondenes church, built of stone in the Gothic style in 1250, and

the Adolf cannon which we find at the fortress. This is the largest cannon that Germans manufactured, and with a shot length of 50 km it defended Rombaksfjorden and Narvik. In Harstad it is possible for groups to take a sailing trip on the schooner Anna Rogde, considered a "national monument" because it is the second oldest schooner still in operation. You can also take the opportunity to go on board the Hurtigruten and sail to Tromso. With this trip you kill two birds with one stone, the experience of sailing on the Hurtigruten and simultaneously enjoying the beautiful scenery. The trip lasts 6 1/2 hours. We pass Senja and make a stop in **Finnsnes** where you can experience how people live in a small coastal community north of the Arctic Circle. We leave the islands over **Tjeldsundbrua**, a suspension bridge that is over 1,000 feet long, and come back to the mainland. The road runs parallel to Ofotfjorden, and on the other side, we can see Narvik.

The city is located 345 km north of the Arctic Circle and 739 km south of North Cape. Narvik, with

Harstad.

Harstad: centre and Trondenes church.

approximately 19,000 residents, is a major hub for road access to Sweden, Islands and north. The city is Norway's second largest port in terms of export capacity.

The city was founded in 1902, 19 years after a Swedish-British company decided to build a port which was free of ice in winter, and where they could export iron ore from the mines in Kiruna in northern Sweden. Construction of Ofotbanen took four years and was the basis for the city's growth. On April 9th, 1940, the city with its strategic port was occupied by the Germans. Allied forces with the French, English, Polish and Norwegian troops counterattacked in the famous battle of Narvik, which was the first Allied victory over Hitler's war machine. The victory was short-lived. On June 8th, the Germans attacked again and occupied the city until the end of the war.

Narvik is today possibly one of the places where the memory of the war is still alive. The War Museum displays interesting models that tell about the battle of Narvik and the German occupation. It also displays sculptures and other items that belonged to the prisoners of war, and a small shrine to the memory of the French forces. In the vicinity there are monuments, memorial stones and several war cemeteries for both the Allied and German soldiers. This reminds us of the scope of this war. For history never to repeat itself, the city erected a Peace Monument depicting six children at play.

The main street in Narvik is the Kongens Gate, which is shared by the

Narvik.

modern port facilities for the loading of iron. This is completely automated with the help of modern technology. Annually around 220 boats are loaded with approximately 14 million tonnes of iron ore. Iron ore is transported daily from Kiruna on13 trains, each with 52 carriages, with ca. 80 tonnes per carriage. The progressive decline in exports of iron has made Narvik find other resources in industry, technology and tourism.

Narvik is a bustling tourist centre. In the summer, the main activities are excursions to the islands, trips on **Ofotbanen** to the Swedish border which is a few miles away, fishing and other outdoor activities. In winter the focus is on ski tourism. Narvik, Northern Norway's most modern ski resort.

Do not forget to pay a visit to the **Ofot Museum**, which depicts Ofotbanen history and the city's strong growth. Take the cable car up to **Fagernesfjellet** which is 656 metres high. The view of both fjords and mountains are incredibly beautiful

in the winter and a dream when the midnight sun shines in the summer. On clear days, far out in the fjord you can make out the silhouettes of the wrecks of two German warships.

Before you go further, you must stop by one of the world's most famous road signs. A total of 22 signs showing the distance from Narvik to the North Pole (2.407 km), Rome (3.978 km), Belgrade (3.957 km), Oslo (1.407 km), etc.

The War Museum in Narvik.

Tromsø.

10. NORTHERN-NORWAY: TROMS AND FINNMARK

Troms County has an area of 26.000 km². It has 159,000 inhabitants and its the largest city is Tromsø. This whole area is still less developed than Nordland. There are important sources of raw materials here, especially minerals, with the thought of further industrial development.

On our way through Troms we pass **Lavangen** and **Bardu** where Norway's largest military base is located, and there are many great opportunities to experience unspoilt nature. The main attractions on this stretch are the Bardu Air Museum, Polar Zoo, where you can see the polar region's most representative species: wolves, lynx, wolverines, caribou, moose, deer, musk ox and arctic foxes.

In **Målselv** municipality is the impressive Målselvfossen, which has one of the world's longest salmon ladders, beautiful areas for hiking and camping areas. We have now reached the **Finnmark plateau** and Sami land. Along E6, we drive past several "siidas". Sami people who live here are nomads, who the summer follow the reindeer and sell handicrafts and souvenirs. The most interesting of these sites is the one in **Balsfjord**.

We drive along the fjord to E8 Tromsø. Here the reflections of the mountains in the fjord can be a magnificent sight. Tromsø is 2.558 km², and is not only the largest municipality, also the largest, northernmost city in the world. It is located at 69° north, the same latitude as Alaska, and has 70,000 inhabitants.

Tromsø is an impressive city in many

Tromsø.

ways. First and foremost because of its location on an island in a fjord surrounded by mountains. To get a good overview of this unique city, it is best to take the cable car up to the Storsteinen, which is 421 metres high. The view is especially beautiful when seen in the midnight sun's magic light, from May 21st to July 23rd. Then you should visit the **Arctic Cathedral**, which has a very beautiful design. It was built by Jan Inge Hovig between 1956 and 1961 and intended as a tribute to the harmonious coexistence between man and nature under these harsh climatic conditions. The church is built of eleven panels laid on top of each other, and has Norway's largest stained glass. You could say that it resembles an iceberg in the polar night, or the keel of a Viking ship.

We cross the bridge over to the island and discover a city full of life,

with lush vegetation (in this regard, we particularly noticed the "Tromsø palm", a species of horsetail that can grow over 4 m high). Besides that, there are pretty houses built in terraces and painted in different colours, and two commercial streets, well-maintained in an old traditional style and full of people as long as the stores are open. Tromsø is also known as the "Paris of the North" - a term from the 1800s because of the so-called "sophisticated" women who were quick to follow the latest women's fashions from Paris. Important polar expeditions have had their origin here, and the city has the world's northernmost university, with 10,000 students who liven up the city in the evening in the pubs and discotheques. In Tromsø, we find **Skarven**, the northernmost and most enjoyable pub. It is located on the

The Artic Cathedral in Tromsø.

fjord, furnished in an exciting way and has a terrace with stunning views. The patio is always crowded when the sun is shining. Find yourself a table inside or out (the view is equally good in both spots), order a Mack beer - the local beer – gull eggs and shrimp, chat a bit with the "natives" or just enjoy the music. At Skarven you can always get the last drink, whether it's midnight sun or the polar night.

Tromsø also has a rich scientific and cultural life. **The university** has a major medical school and the world's most advanced research centre for the study of the upper layers of the atmosphere and the Northern Lights, which in Troms is quite strong. On Fagernes, outside Tromsø, you can see the **Eiscat** radar, the world's most modern radar for studying the Northern Lights. In the Northern Lights Planetarium, which also belongs to the university, you can attend interesting presentations that deal with this phenomenon.

The city has ten museums. Of these we want to mention the **Tromsø University Museum**, with major archaeological and historical collections, and collections associated with Sami culture and animal and plant life. The modern **Polaria** is a centre for experiences related to the polar regions, the world's northernmost **Botanical Garden**, which displays Arctic flora and mountains plants from all over the world, and **Macks Beer Brewery**, which has existed in Northern Norway since 1877. You should not miss the exciting and interesting **Polar Museum**, which tells, in a very interesting way, the story of trappers and hunters who hunted whales and seals on Spitsbergen (Svalbard), the heroic expeditions of Fridtjof Nansen and Otto Sverdrup with the ship Fram and the Amundsen expeditions to the Northwest Passage and the South Pole.

Tromsø is one of the cities in Norway which hosts many festivals, conventions and conferences. In winter, the Northern Lights Festival which marks the end of the dark period and the coming of light, and Film Festival. In summer there is the Døgnvill festival, Beer festival and Midnight Sun Marathon.

Tromsø is also well prepared for life in the northern latitudes. The city is the "gateway" to Svalbard and the Barents Sea. In the harbour is Hurtigruten, fishing boats, marine vessels and research ships. At the busy airport, the large planes of the airlines SAS and Norwegian compete with small aircraft flying between the islands, north or to the Russian border. Although the city is located far to the north the Gulf Stream reduces the cold. Nevertheless, the city is covered with snow and ice in the winter, the record snow fall in Tromsø is 240 cm and was set in April 1997.

During the winter most of the activities are indoors. We can promise you that Tromsø will surprise you with its vibrancy, beauty and intense contrasts. We continue north on County Road 91 to **Breivikeidet**, where we take the ferry over to Ullsfjorden Svensøy. We proceed to **Lyngseidet** traveling across the fjord to **Olderdalen**. This last ferry ride is outstanding. It lasts 40 minutes and crosses three fjords: **Storfjord, Kåfjord** and **Lyngenfjorden,** surrounded by a stunning landscape of mountains, lakes, snow and glaciers. We have come to Lyngen, one of the most stunning mountain landscapes in Northern Norway. You may possibly ask yourself between the mist, wind and salt smell if the mountains are rising up or sinking into the blue sea. We continue on

Polar Centre

The Sealing Ship MS Polstjerna.

E6. The 140 km which are left until we get to Finnmark go through very beautiful scenery, especially when we drive along the eastern shore of Lyngenfjorden. Mountains, reindeer, farms, fishing villages and small towns. As we continue along the fjord, we see shrub vegetation and small, stunted birch trees, but a few metres higher up the landscape it is flat and barren.

By **Bognelv** we drive into **Finnmark**, the country's northernmost county. Finnmark is largest of the counties in area, almost 50,000 km², but the smallest in population (under 75,000). All of Denmark could fit in it! This is the great plateau land with reindeer and a rugged coastline, always subject to the forces of nature. In Finnmark, temperatures can fluctuate wildly. Along the coast, the Gulf Stream provides a relatively mild climate, but in on the Finnmark plateau, temperatures vary from up to 32 degrees in summer to -55 in winter. We are therefore facing a landscape of great contrasts, a wild landscape with a distinctive beauty. The various municipalities in Finnmark today have a somewhat impersonal touch. There's a shopping centre, gas station, bank, church, school and single homes, a result of the region having been destroyed when the Germans withdrew in 1944. We continue on E6 and drive past **Isnestoften**, where there is a large Sami settlement; remnants of the German defences, and continue past **Talvik** and **Kåfjord**, where there are copper mines, and where Professor Kristian Birkeland in 1891 built the first observatory for studying the Northern Lights, which today has been restored. The German battleship Tirpitz was located here until it was damaged in an attack by midget submarines and moved to Tromsø. We now arrive in **Alta** (19,000 inhabitants), Finnmark's largest town. A typical Northern Norwegian municipality, built around an old shopping centre next to the church, and around a newer centre next to the Rica Hotel. Alta is a gathering and selling place for the Sami in Finnmark, and has good road links to Kautokeino, Sweden and Finland. The economic bases of the area are the large slate quarries. The area has grown in recent years, and there has

been some industrial and cultural development. Today, the upper secondary school in Finnmark has over 2,000 students.

The most interesting sight is the **Alta Museum** with a superb collection of petroglyphs. The museum was expanded in 1992 and has a main building with exhibits showing Finnmark's nature, history and natural resources. At the seaside outside the museum, there are paths that take us to one of Europe's most complete collection of petroglyphs. It was included in the UNESCO list of the heritage of humanity in 1985. It is a collection of over 2,500 petroglyphs that are between 6,500 and 2,500 years old, and tells how prehistoric man lived, hunted and fished. There are drawings of reindeer, elk, hunting and fishing scenes, corrals with animals, strange rituals, symbols, all this with Altafjorden as backdrop.

Alta's surroundings are a constant invitation to experience nature up close.

Alta museum.

Petroglyphs at the Alta museum.

We can suggest excursions to the Finnmark plateau, the **Sautso gorge** which is Northern Europe's largest, or boating and fishing on the River Alta. After Alta we come to **Sennalandet**. A typical deserted Finnmark landscape covered with snow and ice eight months of the year, but in summer it is covered with moss, lichen and insects! Sometimes we see one or more reindeer; an occasional house with a snowmobile parked outside, or even a small church. Autumn is the time for berry picking: raspberries, blueberries and cloudberries, Norwegians eat them fresh with cream or milk, or for baking in cakes or, where cloudberries are concerned, making liqueur.

At **Skaidi** we continue on County Road 94 about 60 km west to **Hammerfest**. The world's

Hammerfest.

Polar bear club in Hammerfest.

northernmost city has around 10,000 inhabitants. Hammerfest was burned by the Germans in 1944, and had to be rebuilt. The city hall, sports stadium and the church are some of the interesting buildings. The church has a modern, triangular design, which was designed in 1961 by Hans Magnus. The city also has a busy fishing port, where Hurtigruten makes regular calls. Hammerfest has had a major economic and industrial growth in recent years. The firm Findus has factories here. The city was incidentally the first in the world to have electric street lighting.

The Polar Bear Club is also here. Previously, it was a club for hunters; today the club works for the protection of polar bears and their habitat. The centre has an interesting museum that tells the history of polar bear hunting, shows us how polar bears live, and has the world's largest polar bear skins.

We will also mention Meridianstøtten, erected in the harbour, in memory of the time measurements of the Earth started from here in 1895, with the participation of Danes, Swedes, Russians and Norwegians.

We return to Skaidi, continuing on E6 and come to **Olderfjord** located in a cove in Porsangerfjorden. There is almost no vegetation, only large rocks and a large and desolate landscape.

We continue on the E69 towards North Cape, located on Magerøy, Europe's northernmost point at 71 degrees 10 '21" north., Up to 1999 you had to take a ferry to get here, but now there is a tunnel to **Honningsvåg**, which is the municipality's centre. Below we are exactly half way between the North Pole and Oslo. Magerøy has a pleasant coastal climate thanks to

Honningsvåg.

the Gulf Stream. In winter there are 67 days of "polar night", from November 18th to January 24th and in summer there are 77 days of midnight sun from May 11th to July 31st. There is little vegetation on the island; it is mostly covered by lichen for reindeer grazing who come here in the summer from inner Finnmark. There is also interesting bird cliffs on the island, such as **Gjesværstappen**. Since there is a lot of plankton in the ocean, there is very good fishing in the area. Mostly cod and herring are fished here, and there are also some farms. Sea lions, seals and whales have disappeared from the area.

Most of the 3,000 residents live on the east coast of the island, in Honningsvåg and small fishing villages like Skarsvåg. Honningsvåg is a modern town with a fish freezing

facility and other fishing-related industries, as well as shopping centre, a local newspaper, television station, schools and hotels. In summer the Sami come from Kautokeino and Karasjok with more than 5,000 reindeer that graze here. In the past the reindeer swam in the cold water to the island, but now they are transported over by boat.

The road to **North Cape** was opened in 1956 and was later improved. During the 40 km that separate North Cape from Honningsvåg, we can enjoy a magnificent landscape of bare mountains and rugged coastline.

North Cape is a large rock with a 307 metre drop into the sea. It's like a giant balcony looking out onto the endless ocean and a perfect horizon where sea and sky blend into each other. If we add the midnight sun, magic, strength and beauty, provided the weather conditions are good, we can understand why thousands of visitors come here every year to see this unique "roof of the world".

It is an amazing sight. Huge cliffs above a sea that can prove alternately agitated or calm. Stones, rocks, cairns built by unknown visitors. Some monuments, the strength of the wind, the screams of the birds. Everything is so magnificent that you feel like a microscopic part of the universe's perfect infinity.

There is another good reason that year after year, so many people come to North Cape. In primitive societies, far back in time, religion was tied to the darkness and the light, the symbols of life and death. Primitive man found protection and response in the White Goddess, the Moon. Today's modern man is still looking for the same thing: to get away from darkness and night, the symbols of death, and to seek eternal life in the light and day, in the sunshine that lasts 24 hours a day, so that you can go from one day to the next without it getting dark, as a symbol of life. It might be that North Cape, in addition to its beauty, is the large balcony where you can be immortalized, just like primitive man, in the light and in life. The rock has had this power of attraction since time immemorial. The North Cape was discovered and named by Richard Chancellor in 1553. Christian IV sailed around the Cape in 1599. In the 1600's the Italian Negri came here, and in 1798 Acerbi said in full admiration: "I feel like a creator." Other famous visitors were Prince Louis of Orleans (1798), later King Louis-Philippe of France, Thomas Carlyle, King Oscar II, Emperor Wilhelm II, and even Siam's King Chulalongkorn.

The North Cape Museum in Honningsvåg.

At the Tourist Centre, which is cut into the rock, we can see the midnight sun through the windows. We can buy souvenirs, drink coffee or soft drinks, dine, write and send postcards with postmarks from the North Cape. But by all means do not miss the film about the North Cape and Magerøy which is shown over five screens in "Supervideograph". From there you can go down to an exhibition of historical figures who visited the Cape, on to the chapel (small but beautiful) and to Kong Oscars Hall, which has an open balcony to the sea and horizon. Finally, we end at

the Nordkapp club, which is happy to welcome new members.

From North Cape E69 and after Olderfjord, E6 go along Porsangerfjorden towards Lakselv and Karasjok. E6 continues along the Finnish border and the river Anarjokka, to **Tana bru** and **Kirkenes**, almost at the Russian border. E75 goes to **Vadsø** which is the regional centre and **Vardø**, Norway's easternmost town. From Olderfjord Vardø or Kirkenes it is 415 km between fjords, rivers and a landscape that is becoming more and more typical of inland areas.

The North Cape.   *Kirkeporten, the North Cape.*

Kirkenes.

Vardø.

Winter day in Øvre Pasvik National Park.

South of Kirkenes FV 885 goes into a land pocket between Russia and Finland, and after about 100 km we come to the **Øvre Pasvik National Park**, which has an abundance of wildlife and much vegetation. Another nice excursion is to take FV 886 to the northeast. After 57 km we reach the border station **Grense-Jakobselv**, where King Oscar II had a chapel built in 1869.

King Oscar II's chapel at Grense-Jakobselv.

Kautokeino.

Sami land

E6, which in some places is built over old reindeer migration routes, takes us into the inner Finnmark, to the Finnmark plateau. We are back on the big plateau with lichen, moss and reindeer. The trees are small, twisted and far apart. Here are the municipalities of Karasjok and Kautokeino on the Norwegian side and Inari on the Finnish side.

Karasjok, which means "the river that turns" in Sami, has nearly 3,000 residents. The area's centre consists of a shopping mall, a gas station, a school and a church. Among the Sami institutions, we particularly want to point out the Sami Parliament, the Sami collections and Sami Art Centre. The Sami collections show Sami culture and lifestyle. There is also a restaurant built in typical style, and a hall where you can see the short film "*Gammen*" (the hut), as well as a store where you can buy beautiful jewellery, amulets, drums and knives.

30 km east is the Finnish border, and 130 km southwest is **Kautokeino**, where reindeer breeders meet. With its 9.700 km² is Norway's largest municipality, which still only has just over 3,000 residents. It has a beautiful church built in 1958, after the previous one was burned during the War. Kautokeino also has a modern culture that won the Norwegian architectural award in 1987. This is the home of the Sami theatre. We would also recommend a visit to the store Juhl, which sells beautiful Sami jewellery and also contains an art gallery.
Kautokeino also hosts the Easter Festival, with big Sami weddings, reindeer and sledding races and

other competitions, exhibitions of handicrafts, etc. There we can see the Sami in their fine costumes.

From Kautokeino it is not far to the Finnish border. In Northern Finland, 150 km from Karasjok, is the third of the Sami municipalities, **Inari**. Here we find Sami's famous holy lake Inarijärvi, the fifth largest lake in Finland, as well as the fascinating museum Siida, which shows how the Sami people have existed throughout history, their way of life and the environment, all in an interesting and excellent presentation. It is suggested that you go for a walk in the woods to get to know the various Sami construction methods. It's worth it, but there are a lot of mosquitoes, so take precautions.

Sami in traditional costumes.

Juhls Silver Gallery in Kautokeino.

Longyearbyen, Svalbard.

11. SVALBARD AND SPITSBERGEN

The Svalbard archipelago is located in the Barents Sea 640 km north of Finnmark and 1,300 km from the North Pole, between 74 and 81 degrees north. It consists of nine islands, the largest of which is **Spitsbergen**. Overall, the archipelago has an area of 61.020 km². Often we stop at Jan Mayen which is 377 km², although the island does not formally belong to Svalbard. Jan Mayen is an important meteorological station, and has Norway's only active volcano.

In Svalbard, there is an international population, most Norwegians and Russians. Both Norway, Russia, Denmark and Sweden wanted sovereignty over the islands, but it was given to Norway under the Treaty of Paris of 1920.

The group of island is a natural paradise that has remained untouched due to its isolated location and low temperatures ranging between -14° C in winter and 6° C in summer. There have been winters with temperatures down to -30° C for long periods, and in 1986 the temperature was as low as -46° C. 60% of the islands are covered with rocks and glaciers. At this latitude the sun is gone from October 27th to February 15th, with full "polar night" from November 14th to January 29th. The midnight sun shines from April 20th to August 22nd.

Hjortefjellet and Longyearbyen.

11. Svalbard and Spitsbergen

This world of ice, rocks, cliffs and sea have been preserved as a real natural paradise. The islands have 165 different plant species, more than 40 varieties of birds, and a variety of marine and land mammals. Polar bears, arctic foxes, more than 10,000 caribou, seals and walruses. For the preservation of this unique world two national parks have been created as well as several nature reserves.

The islands were opened to tourists in 1990. There are eight hotels and a camping ground on Spitsbergen, but where tourists are allowed to go and not go is strictly regulated. The largest settlement is **Longyearbyen**, located by Isfjorden and has 2,000 inhabitants (2008), mostly Norwegians. Here you will find the interesting Svalbard Museum. The settlement of **Barentsburg** has 950 inhabitants, mostly Russians, who are involved in mining.

" Beware of polar bear", warning sign, Svalbard.

Polar bear, Svalbard.

Baby seal greets its mother.

The thing that attracts people to these islands is their unique and magnificent, untouched nature. There are several travel agencies that organize trips here, both in summer and winter. There is skiing, snowmobiling, trekking, hiking among the Arctic flora and fauna, boat excursions on the fjord to the foot of the great glaciers, glacier trekking, mines tours, safaris for polar bears footprints, staying in an igloo, dog sled excursion, short and long boat trips around the various islands, kayaking and trips by motorboat and visiting the bird cliffs. A standing invitation to experience the adventure of truly magnificent environment.

Expedition trip, Svalbard.

Text: Salvador Sala
Edited by: Andreas Kiil
March 2013

The following photographers,
in association with Normanns Kunstforlag, contributed their work:
Anders Wesnes, Andreas Kiil, Arctic Photo, Are K. Haram, Arne Lunde,
Arne Normann, Arnstein Rønning, Bjarne Riesto, Bjørnar Ingulfsen
Foto, Bård Løken / Samfoto, Bård Løken / Scanpix, Baard Næss /
Samfoto, Carl Wijting, Dieter Muessler, Dino Sassi, Elinor Vikås, Finn
Loftesnes, Fjellanger Widerøe, Flickr, Georg Bangjord / Samfoto, Giulio
Bolognesi, Hans de Zeeuw, Hans Petter Sørensen, Harald B. Valder-
haug, Helge Ask, Herbert Czoschke, Husmo Foto, Ibsen museet, Jan
Horn, Jan Lykke, Jøran Solnes Skaar, Karlsen Anette / Scanpix, Kjell
Narvestad, Kjell Solheimsnes, Kon-Tiki museet, Maciek Lulko, Marco
Boella, Munch-museet, N.F. / A.L. Reinsfelt, Nadia Norskott, Nasjonal-
galleriet, Nikon / R. Krasnig, Norsk Bildebyrå / Torbjørn Moen, Norsk
husflidslag, OFK Bildearkiv, Per Andersen, Per Ivar Somby, Robert Kirk
Hamilton, Rune Baashus, Samfoto, Scanpix, Sebastian Hoppe, Siro
Leonardi, Steinar Vikås, Torben Brenden Pedersen, Trond Tandberg,
Trond Aalde, Trygve Gulbrandsen, Trym Ivar Bergsmo / Samfoto, Tycho
Anker-Nilssen, Upper Namsen Fishing, Urpo Tarnanen, Willy Haraldsen,
Willy Kittelsen, Geir Benden / www.arctic-circle.no, www.nettfoto.no,
www.seafood.no, Ørjan Skoglund

Translated by Language Power International AS